Indochina Monographs

Strategy and Tactics
by
Col. Hoang Ngoc Lung

U.S. ARMY CENTER OF MILITARY HISTORY

WASHINGTON, D.C.

Library of Congress Cataloging in Publication Data

Lung, Hoang Ngoc.
  Strategy and tactics.

  (Indochina monographs)
  1. Vietnamese Conflict, 1961-1975. 2. Strategy.
3. Tactics. I. Title. II. Series.
U742.L86   959.704'34   79-607102

This book is not copyrighted and may be reproduced in whole or in part without consulting the publisher

Reprinted 1984

CMH PUB 92-15

Indochina Monographs

This is one of a series originally published in limited quantity in 1980 by the U.S. Army Center of Military History. The continuous demand for these monographs has prompted reprinting. They were written by officers who held responsible positions in the Cambodian, Laotian, and South Vietnamese armed forces during the war in Indochina. The General Research Corporation provided writing facilities and other necessary support under an Army contract with the Center of Military History. The monographs were not edited or altered and reflect the views of their authors--not necessarily those of the U.S. Army or the Department of Defense. The authors were not attempting to write definitive accounts but to set down how they saw the war in Southeast Asia.

These works should provide useful source materials for serious historians pending publication of the Center's more definitive series, the U.S. Army in Vietnam.

DOUGLAS KINNARD
Brigadier General, USA (Ret)
Chief of Military History

INDOCHINA MONOGRAPHS

TITLES IN THE SERIES
(title--author/s--LC Catalog Card)

The Cambodian Incursion--Brig. Gen. Tran Dinh Tho--79-21722	CMH PUB 92-4
The Easter Offensive of 1972--Lt. Gen. Ngo Quang Truong--79-20551	CMH PUB 92-13
The General Offensives of 1968-69--Col. Hoang Ngoc Lung--80-607931	CMH PUB 92-6
Intelligence--Col. Hoang Ngoc Lung--81-10844/AACR2	CMH PUB 92-14
The Khmer Republic at War and the Final Collapse--Lt. Gen. Sak Sutsakhan--79-607776	CMH PUB 92-5
Lam Son 719--Maj. Gen. Nguyen Duy Hinh--79-607101	CMH PUB 92-2
Leadership--General Cao Van Vien--80-607941	CMH PUB 92-12
Pacification--Brig. Gen. Tran Dinh Tho--79-607913	CMH PUB 92-11
RLG Military Operations and Activities in the Laotian Panhandle--Brig. Gen. Soutchay Vongsavanh--81-10934/AACR2	CMH PUB 92-19
The RVNAF--Lt. Gen. Dong Van Khuyen--79-607963	CMH PUB 92-7
RVNAF and U.S. Operational Cooperation and Coordination--Lt. Gen. Ngo Quang Truong--79-607170	CMH PUB 92-16
RVNAF Logistics--Lt. Gen. Dong Van Khuyen--80-607117	CMH PUB 92-17
Reflections on the Vietnam War--General Cao Van Vien and Lt. Gen. Dong Van Khuyen--79-607979	CMH PUB 92-8
The Royal Lao Army and U.S. Army Advice and Support--Maj. Gen. Oudone Sananikone--79-607054	CMH PUB 92-10
The South Vietnamese Society--Maj. Gen. Nguyen Duy Hinh and Brig. Gen. Tran Dinh Tho--79-17694	CMH PUB 92-18
Strategy and Tactics--Col. Hoang Ngoc Lung--79-607102	CMH PUB 92-15
Territorial Forces--Lt. Gen. Ngo Quang Truong--80-15131	CMH PUB 92-9
The U.S. Adviser--General Cao Van Vien, Lt. Gen. Ngo Quang Truong, Lt. Gen. Dong Van Khuyen, Maj. Gen. Nguyen Duy Hinh, Brig. Gen. Tran Dinh Tho, Col. Hoang Ngoc Lung, and Lt. Col. Chu Xuan Vien--80-607108	CMH PUB 92-1
Vietnamization and the Cease-Fire--Maj. Gen. Nguyen Duy Hinh--79-607982	CMH PUB 92-3
The Final Collapse--General Cao Van Vien--81-607989	CMH PUB 90-26

Preface

During the war years, the Republic of Vietnam and the United States pursued a common goal; their armed forces fought against the same enemy, under the same campaign plan, with the same weapon systems, and in the same environment.

The strategic approaches to fighting this war, however, evolved through several stages depending on the enemy's kind of warfare and force structure; so did the tactics designed to counter his large-unit and guerrilla activities. This monograph endeavors, therefore, to trace back and evaluate our strategic alternatives at each stage of the war and the evolving tactics employed, with particular emphasis on the period of American withdrawal and reduced support.

In the preparation of this monograph, I have expressly confined my discussions of strategy to its military aspect. While this conforms to the limited scope of a military subject, the encompassing nature of strategy, especially one conceived to face the enemy's approach to total war, implies that for a better understanding of military strategy, the interplay of social, political, and economic factors should also be brought in as a backdrop. Therefore, wherever appropriate, I have found it necessary to place strategic discussions in the total war context.

I am indebted to General Cao Van Vien, Chairman of the Joint General Staff, Lieutenant General Dong Van Khuyen, Chief of Staff — under whom I served several years as Assistant Chief of Staff J2, JGS — and Brigadier General Tran Dinh Tho, Assistant Chief of Staff J3, JGS, for their valuable comments. Lieutenant General Ngo Quang Truong,

Commanding General of I Corps and Major General Nguyen Duy Hinh, Commander of the 3d Infantry Division, contributed thoughtful remarks and the practical view of field commanders.

Finally, I am particularly indebted to Lieutenant Colonel Chu Xuan Vien and Ms. Pham Thi Bong. Lt. Colonel Vien, the last Army Attache serving at the Vietnamese Embassy in Washington, D.C., has done a highly professional job of translating and editing. Ms. Bong, a former Captain in the Republic of Vietnam Armed Forces and also a former member of the Vietnamese Embassy Staff, spent long hours typing, editing and in the administrative preparation of my manuscript in final form.

McLean, Virginia
10 July 1978

Hoang Ngoc Lung
Colonel, ARVN

Contents

Chapter		Page
I.	INTRODUCTION	1
	North Vietnam's National Objectives and Basic Strategy	1
	South Vietnamese National Objectives and Basic Strategy	5
II.	EARLY STRATEGIES	10
	Pacification	10
	Strategy Under the First Republic of South Vietnam	14
	Improving Communications and Control	20
	Strategic Hamlets	23
III.	STRATEGY DURING THE PERIOD OF U.S. PARTICIPATION	33
	Pacification and Rural Development	34
	Operation Phoenix	41
	Vietnamization	47
	The Problem of Survival	57
IV.	UNITED STATES' INFLUENCE ON REPUBLIC OF VIETNAM'S STRATEGY	62
	American Influence in the Pre-Intervention Period	62
	Americanization	70
	American Influence After Withdrawal	75
V.	THE TACTICS OF THE REPUBLIC OF VIETNAM ARMED FORCES	77
	The First Steps	77
	A New Direction	81
	Modified Tactics and Their Effects	85
	Solving Difficult Tactical Problems	88
	Night Operations	89
	Cordon and Search	92
	Defense Against Sappers	95
	Defense Against Shelling	101

Chapter	Page
VI. SPECIAL U.S. COMBAT TECHNIQUES	105
B-52 Bombers	106
Defoliation	111
The Rome Plow	115
Riot Control Agents	120
VII. STRATEGIES AND TACTICS OF NORTH VIETNAM	122
The Military Art	123
Common Communist Tactics	126
VIII. OBSERVATIONS AND CONCLUSIONS	130
GLOSSARY	138

Illustrations

Vietnamese Rangers Boarding U.S. Army H-21 Helicopters in an Operation Against Viet Cong Bases in the Plain of Reeds in 1962	17
Ranger Observation Post Near Trung Lap, May 1962	18
Watchtower Under Construction in a Strategic Hamlet, 1962	30
Women of the Civil Guard at Hoa Cam	31
Women in the Local Militia in Military Drill, 1962	32
Regular ARVN Infantrymen of the 1st Battalion, 33d Infantry, 21st Division During an Operation in the Mekong Delta, An Xuyen Province, 1967	37
Vietnamization: 105-mm Howitzers of the 9th U.S. Infantry Division are Turned Over to the ARVN 213th Artillery Battalion at Can Tho, 26 April 1969	48
Sentry Post Manned by a Popular Forces Unit Guarding a Bridge Over a Canal, 1970	51
Three Wickham Trolleys on the Saigon-Bien Hoa Railway, 1965	67
Soviet Assault Rifles (AK-47) Captured During the 1970 Cambodian Incursion on Public Display	74
An ARVN Airborne Battalion Moves Through Tall Grass Toward a Bamboo Thicket in Search of the Enemy, 1962	83
An Ex-Sapper Demonstrates Infiltrating Through Barbed Wire and a Mine Field at Long Binh, August 1969	99
Rome Plows Clearing Brush and Leveling Terrain, 1970	117

CHAPTER I

Introduction

North Vietnam's National Objectives and Basic Strategy

The Geneva Accords concluded on 20 July 1954 divided Vietnam into two zones clearly demarcated along the 17th parallel. The North adopted a single-party, totalitarian, socialist regime while the South had a nationalist government in which pluralism and free enterprise were encouraged. The war that lasted from 1946 to 1954 had come to an end, and the political solution provided for by the Geneva Accords called for a general election to be held two years later to reunify the country.

Peace was necessary for North Vietnam to rebuild its society and heal the wounds of war; in the preceding years the North was the scene of the heaviest fighting of the war. The economy was a shambles; agricultural production fell short of the people's requirements (the annual shortage amounted to approximately 250 thousand tons of rice) and created a need for imports. Highways, bridges and railroads were in bad condition. Light industries, still in their infancy, were dispersed throughout the country. North Vietnam's military forces, which had so decisively defeated the French at Dien Bien Phu, were strong but in urgent need of reorganization; they had been expanded greatly but irregularly during the war.

The task of rebuilding the country and consolidating its political power required more than two years for the northern leadership to accomplish. This is why South Vietnam's rejection of the 1956 general election occasioned only a diplomatic, though strong, protest from the north.[1] North Vietnam's strategy during this period put emphasis on strengthening the society of the North rather than on taking action in the South. On *Tet* (New Year) 1957, Ho Chi Minh explained this strategy to cadres that had been regrouped from the South:

> "To build a long-lasting building, we must lay a solid foundation. The North is the foundation, the taproot of the struggle to liberate and reunify our country. Therefore, what we are doing in the North is for the purpose of strengthening both North and South. Thus, our work here is like the struggle in the South, for the South, and for all of Vietnam."

Meanwhile, the situation was deteriorating day by day for the Communists in South Vietnam. Out of 50,000 Communist cadres left behind in the South, only 10,000 members were still active by 1959. The remaining 40,000 either rallied to the South Vietnamese government or simply vanished; that is, moved away and quietly stopped operating for the Communists. It came to a point where a district level Communist cadre for example, had to serve both as District and Village Commissar. Sometimes there were no officers at all.

The growing South Vietnamese strength eventually forced the North to reexamine its strategy. In May 1959 at a general meeting of its Central Executive Committee, the Workers' (Communist) Party of North Vietnam decided upon the liberation of South Vietnam. The first step would be to infiltrate the South with cadres that had gone north in 1954. In order to do this, a logistics system would be required. Consequently, the North Vietnamese Army established Group 559 with the mission of directing and supporting the infiltration of men, weapons, ammunition and explosives into the South.

---

[1] A communique issued by the South Vietnamese government on April 6, 1956 stated "The Government of the RVN respects the present state of peace. As has been stated many times, the Government of RVN desires to seek reunification of the country through peaceful means, especially through truly democratic and free elections when such free conditions obtain."

In September 1960, during its third General Assembly, North Vietnam's Workers' Party officially decided that the twofold strategic goal of the North would be (1) to carry on the building of socialism in the North and (2) to start the revolutionary war of liberation in the South. The liberation of the South was perceived as a long-term, arduous struggle at all levels. The aim was to establish, strengthen, and develop a popular front in the South that gave the appearance of a spontaneous movement by the people to overthrow the government. For that purpose, the National Liberation Front of South Vietnam officially came into being on 20 December 1960.

The military strategy devised by North Vietnam called for a people's war to be fought through three stages: the stage of contention; the stage of equilibrium; and the general counteroffensive. In the stage of contention the strategy is defensive during which violent attacks on government installations are followed by immediate withdrawals to prepared positions. Guerrilla warfare is the dominant characteristic. In the stage of equilibrium, the insurgents have become as powerful as the government force, but remain on the strategic defensive while preparing for the stage of the general counteroffensive by making constant attacks to wear down the enemy and retake lost positions. In the final stage, the counteroffensive, the enemy is forced to defend and retreat in the face of mobile warfare, supported by the guerrillas who themselves are gradually transformed into mobile, regular formations.[2]

With this three-stage strategy as the framework, the Northern leadership promulgated a five-step plan in 1959 for the execution of the war against the South. (There was a doctrinal preference among the Communist ideologues to express all important endeavors in terms of five steps, as in five year economic plans, etc.) Step one provided for propaganda activity to lay the groundwork for the struggle. Step two was the organization of guerrilla forces and the establishment of base areas. In stage three the guerrilla units begin their local attacks. Stage

---

[2] For a full discussion of this three-stage strategy, see Truong Chinh, _Primer for Revolt_, Frederic A. Praeger, New York, 1963.

four called for more vigorous attacks and for the organization of regular forces. Finally, stage five was the large-scale counteroffensive by the regular forces.

The leaders and soldiers who were to carry out the strategy in the South were former Communist cadres and soldiers who had gone north in 1954. Travelling in small groups of 40 to 50, and later in larger groups of 300 to 500, they began infiltrating in 1959 following land routes leading from North Vietnam's Military Region 4 through lower Laos into Quang Tri and Quang Nam in the First Military Region and Kontum in the Second Military Region of the Republic of Vietnam.

Sea routes were utilized only by cadres on special missions in the South, such as intelligence personnel, and for transporting arms, ammunition and explosives. The fifteen vessels intercepted by the South in 1963 provided a general picture of the level of sea infiltration.

Once in the South, these infiltrators were sent to Communist-organized areas in accordance with needs and priorities, where they began to assemble regular armed units. In time these units grew from company size to battalions, and in 1961 the first two Communist regiments were organized in South Vietnam. At the same time, Communist guerrillas and their supporting infrastructure were developed, reaching a strength of 20,000 personnel in 1961. By 1963 nearly all of the Southern cadres had been returned to the South and North Vietnam began to infiltrate Northern cadres and troops.

At the end of 1964, taking advantage of the deterioration of the military and security situation caused by a period of political turmoil in the South, North Vietnam dispatched entire main force regiments southward. These regular units retained their unit integrity and the war had already been advanced from stage two to stage three. During the battle of Pleime in the highlands of the Second Military Region in October 1965, the 325th North Vietnamese Division was involved.

South Vietnamese National Objectives and Basic Strategy

Although North Vietnam in the post-Geneva era encountered numerous difficulties, South Vietnam was beset with even greater political problems as internal struggles wrecked the country. The situation was serious enough to prompt foreign observers to predict the demise of South Vietnam within two years after Geneva.

The Nationalist Army of Vietnam was in the hands of a Chief of the General Staff, Major General Nguyen Van Hinh, who was in open and hostile opposition to the government. The military units of the *Hoa Hao* and *Cao Dai* religious sects, as well as the National Police Force which was controlled by the *Binh Xuyen*, carved out their own fiefdoms and enjoyed near autonomy in their regions.[3]

After restoring the authority of the government and regaining control of the armed forces (Major General Hinh was replaced by Major General Le Van Ty) the government of Ngo Dinh Diem proclaimed the founding of the First Republic of South Vietnam on 26 October 1955. President Diem espoused the doctrine of personalism as a response to Communist dogma and embarked on a reorganization of the forces to meet the threat of invasion from the North.

In addition to internal strife, the new South Vietnamse regime was faced with tough problems of nation-building and the ever-present threat of North Vietnamese aggression. This threat weighed heavily on the minds of South Vietnamese leaders especially after President Diem flatly refused reunification through general elections. The fact was the defense posture of the South was so weak and its geographical position so vulnerable that North Vietnam had all the chances of success if it decided to strike.

South Vietnam borders on North Vietnam to the north, Laos and Cambodia to the west, and the South China Sea to the east. It extends 920 km from the 17th parallel to the north to Cape Ca Mau in the South. At its narrowest it is only 59 km wide; at its widest, 460 km. There are 2,400 km of coastline. Two thirds of South Vietnam consist of high plateaus with

---

[3] *Binh Xuyen* was a society of organized crime that gained exceptional power under the French who permitted it to operate without serious opposition in the Saigon area in exchange for its support against the Viet Minh.

mountains rising to 2,841 meters; dense jungles offer concealment to invading forces. Plains take up the remaining one-third of the land area, the best known being the Mekong Delta, the water-logged rice basket of the South. Waterways navigable to sampans cover 2,080 km while 14,400 km of highways and 1,440 km of railroad form the main arteries of the transportation network. These geographical aspects meant that only a defense in depth was a feasible strategy for South Vietnam, and such a defense would require a large force with superior mobility.

The South's population in 1954 of over 14 million included about 70,000 people from 20 ethnic tribes living in the highlands, 900,000 Chinese concentrated mainly in Cholon, and 400,000 Cambodians in the Mekong Delta.

One significant characteristic of the South's population was the great differences in material well-being and political attitudes between the country people and the city dwellers. Leading a poverty-striken life, peasants had no choice but to adopt a passive attitude toward the war and submit to the direct control of the winning side, be it Nationalist or Communist. This fact was an extremely important factor in shaping the South's strategic defensive thinking, which included building and maintaining area defenses through a network of military fortifications and outposts.

National authority resides in the dual concept of territory and people. The jungles, although part of the territory, harbor little or no population, and therefore command less interest than populated areas and administrative units such as hamlets, villages, districts, and provinces. This explain why during the general offensive of the summer of 1972, the South was determined to recapture the provincial capital of Quang Tri, although it had then been reduced to a huge pile of rubble.

The concept of territorial protection and area defense became a strategic goal in the South's determination to withstand the North's aggressive military designs, to eliminate subversive activities within the South, and to build the republic. In other words, the objectives were survival and independence. In every political situation these remained the two most important objectives of the South.

The South's national goals and strategy were based on the assumption that full American support would be available until proven unnecessary.

This assistance was perceived as being part of the United States strategy which followed the end of World War II with respect to the containment of Communism in Asia as well as in Europe. The South regarded itself as a bastion of the Free World in its effort to resist the Communists.

To carry out the national defense effort, the armed forces of the Republic of Vietnam were organized, trained and operated along conventional lines. This conventional form of the armed forces was apparent when the first South Vietnamese Army was established on 11 May 1950 with a strength of 60,000 men, half of whom were in the regular forces and the other half in auxiliary forces.

The first military officers were trained in local military schools and from 1950 on at the National Military Academy at Dalat. In 1951 the first classes of reserve officers began training in Nam Dinh and Thu Duc. The program of instruction was based on French training methodology and tactical doctrine. Organization of the military units as well as their armaments and equipment were also French. The inevitable result was that this conventional character of the armed forces had a profound influence on the subsequent conduct of the war since its military leaders were trained in conventional tactics. When the U.S. Military Assistance Advisory Group (MAAG) was established in 1956 it continued the French practice of training the regular forces for conventional warfare. The tactics and techniques that American advisors passed on to Vietnamese officers were those that had been learned during World War II or in the Korean Conflict and were thus confined to conventional warfare. Although many Vietnamese officers had fought the Viet Minh, which required the use of unconventional methods, the doctrine upon which all training and operations were based in Republic of Vietnam Armed Forces (RVNAF) continued to be that of conventional war. Even though the battlefield conditions seemed to demand a doctrinal change, this was never accomplished because the security situation—the press of daily operational requirements—never gave the RVNAF time to work out a more suitable doctrine.

While the period from 1954 to 1959 was sufficient for the North to strengthen its internal political system and armed forces, the same period saw the South torn by dissention and weakened by political instability. The aborted coup of 11 November 1960, attempted by three paratroop battalions, set a precedent for the repeated use of the armed forces to seize power. Such attempts were successful twice — during the revolution of 11 November 1963 and the *coup* of 30 January 1964 — and forced South Vietnamese leaders to keep a close watch over the armed forces, to personally appoint and supervise the commanders of elite general reserve units such as the Airborne and Marine Divisions as well as the commanders of the key infantry divisions stationed in the Third and Fourth Military Regions.

The fear of *coups* affected the attitudes and methods of control used by all presidents and chiefs-of-state (except for the civilian Chief-of-State Phan Khac Suu who enjoyed no real authority); they insisted on the power to appoint commanders of corps and divisions mainly on the basis of personal loyalty, and required that direct orders from the Independence Palace were necessary for any significant deployments of units, especially those from the general reserve and those stationed around the City of Saigon.

The pervasive presidential distrust of the military eroded the armed forces' efficiency and created factionalism in the RVNAF. Military leaders at all levels were frequently preoccupied with internal problems and consequently had little time to study the enemy situation. Politics invaded the military and it was not the kind of beneficial, political consciousness that all patriotic soldiers should have, but the politics of survival of the particular regime in power at the time. The true mission of the armed forces, to defeat Communist aggression, was repeatedly neglected in favor of the unspoken concern to prevent an overthrow of the government.

Building political strength through motivating the people's participation in national defense, originated during the First Republic, was pursued as a national goal by every subsequent South Vietnamese administration. The concept of popular self-defense, aided by military and paramilitary forces, was aimed at establishing and maintaining security, which was the basic condition for realizing political, economic and social objectives. This concept, the implementation of which kept changing with new experiences and increased American support, emerged under various guises: Strategic Hamlets, New Life Hamlets, Pacification, and Rural Construction and Development. But the end always remained popular participation in and support of the national policy to confront the Communists in the military, political, economic, and social areas; to confront the enemy in two fundamental aspects of the people's war waged in the South by the Communists: a popular war and a total war.

The people's self-defense capability was an essential complement to the military strategy which relied increasingly on firepower and movement, and the tactics designed to produce them. The people's self-defense capability was necessary to alleviate the shortage of military personnel and to establish the favorable strength ratio demanded by a counter-insurgency situation. This ratio had been determined by Emperor Napoleon as being ten-to-one; experience obtained in the wars in Greece and Malaysia confirmed a similar ratio. In Vietnam, however, the most favorable friendly-to-enemy ratio, which was achieved before American and Free World forces withdrew, was only five-to-one.

But even if we were unable to attract the population to our side in numbers sufficient to provide the theoretical ratio of forces we thought we needed, we still endeavored to separate the population from the enemy so that he could not exploit it for his own purposes. If this strategy succeeded, many of the people would support and defend the Republic, others would be passive but contribute no resources to the enemy, while the regular forces with United States support would eject the invading armies of the North.

CHAPTER II

Early Strategies

Pacification

Pacification was not a new concept for dealing with insurgency. Pacification strategies were applied by the French soon after 1963 when French forces undertook the conquest of Indochina. These strategies called for three phases:

Phase 1: Launch lightning attacks on the enemy's sanctuaries throughout the land in order to destroy his main force and to secure key areas.

Phase 2: Set up defensive positions in occupied territories and start local government functioning.

Phase 3: From controlled areas, launch military operations in order to expand pacified areas and activate civil guard units and village councils in order to strengthen control of rural areas.

During the First Indochina War of 1946-1954, the French put pacification strategies into effect again but applied them in varying degrees and permutations in North, Central, and South Vietnam. In the North, the French initially struck only in the highlands where key Viet Minh commands were located and, except for Son Tay Province, neglected pacification in the plains. Only in early 1948, after their attempts in the highlands had been defeated, did the French initiate their pacification effort in the Red River Delta. The provinces of Hung Yen and Thai Binh were the last occupied by French forces at the end of 1949 and the stiff reaction of the Viet Minh in the Delta eventually reversed the gains the French had made in two years.

The French pacification effort in the Red River Delta was hopelessly flawed; it could not attract the popular support that was essential for success in this densely populated region simply because it was pure French and not Vietnamese. On the other hand, since the Viet Minh had determined that North Vietnam was their main battlefield, they considered it vital that they secure the support and resources of the Delta for the Viet Minh. Therefore, the Viet Minh were vigorous in opposing the French in the Delta and they were able to secure at least the passive support from the people they needed for success.

Finally in 1951, the Vietnamese Governor of North Vietnam persuaded the French to permit him to organize the first Vietnamese pacification effort. Four *Groupe Administratif Militaire Operationel (GAMO)* were formed to carry out the program. The groups had the mission of replacing the military units in newly liberated areas, maintaining law and order, and establishing local government at the grass-roots level. Each group was organized and directed by a prominent Vietnamese with political prestige among the populace; he was usually a member of the nationalist *Dai Viet* Party. Each group consisted of 60 members; there was an administrative team, a military team, a health and welfare team, and an information team. As soon as the group arrived in a newly occupied area, the administrative team began organizing civilian life and surveying the people's needs. The military team combed the area to weed out enemy agents and insure security. The health and welfare team distributed medicines and cared for the sick. The information team, in cooperation with other teams, conducted information sessions to educate the people on the policies of the nationalist government.

The GAMOs achieved respectable success in that they were able to gain the people's sympathy through the Vietnamese nationalist character of their operations. However, with only four GAMOs for the entire North, their operations were limited and the high level of fighting and an ever-worsening military and security situation severely curtailed their activities.

In South Vietnam, pacification was systematically carried out. The plan was based on the old three-stage French program with a few modifications: the initial stage called for repelling the enemy regular forces and destroying their base areas. The second stage consisted of defending territorial gains by setting up military posts along new security belts. The third stage was a period of consolidation, restoring normal life by establishing rural administrative units and organizing the hamlet militia to maintain security of occupied areas.

In 1947 the French assigned to a Vietnamese-French officer, Colonel LeRoy, the task of pacifying the Mekong Delta provinces of My Tho and Ben Tre. He was successful in repelling and controlling the Viet Minh military units but failed to gain genuine popular support because of his cruelties and excesses. Pacification was conceived by him as follows:

> "Pacification is a combination of cruel action and overt and covert political action. On the one hand, it involves commando pursuits and keeping close tabs on the guerrillas; the deployment of an extensive network of informers and the severe repression of villagers or persons who harbor and supply Viet Minh elements. On the other hand, it involves building roads, holding markets, opening schools, erecting dispensaries, helping the people to farm new land, etc."[1]

In 1952, the French began to turn over military control of the territory to the Vietnamese Armed Forces with the expectation that Vietnamese territorial commands would be able to carry out pacification more effectively than French forces. Pacification measures applied included: (1) making a careful and thorough census and screening the population living in controlled areas; (2) bringing paramilitary forces up to strength to enable them to perform security duty in the villages; (3) turning over to these forces a number of minor military posts, thus alleviating the burden on regular forces; and (4) consolidating strike forces and assigning them to mobile duty.

Each sector (the sector was the military division conterminous with the province) was authorized a strike force of 300 men. Some sectors were joined for military operations into sector groups and in that case a strike force of 400 men was authorized. In some regions where the Viet Cong threat was serious enough, military zones were designated and these zones had strike forces authorized 800 men.

---

[1] The Armed Forces of the Republic of Vietnam in the Formative Years, 1946-1955 published by J-5, Joint General Staff RVNAF, 1972, p. 62.

A system of defenses was organized to pacify each province. For example, Go Cong and Ben Tre Provinces in the Delta had a system composed of 1,500 individual sites, such as outposts and watchtowers. The force manning these positions and furnishing the strike forces was 14,800 men, including 1,300 regulars, 6,000 auxiliaries, and 7,500 rural militia.

Le Duan, Chairman of the Viet Cong Administrative Committee for the South, wrote about this situation as follows:

> "While the enemy is active, we are passive because he has divided and surrounded us with an intricate system of fortifications and watchtowers along arteries of communication and deep into rural areas."[2]

Although pacification plans were in effect throughout Vietnam during the war years 1946-1954, success was achieved only in South Vietnam where the influence of the French and the Vietnamese government was greatest among the population and where the enemy forces were weakest. By contrast, pacification failed utterly in North and Central Vietnam because it was not pursued vigorously and was not anchored on a political base capable of attracting the people's allegiance.

Finally, in 1953, the French transfered two northern provinces — Hung Yen and Bui Chu — to Vietnamese command for the purposes of pacification. Vietnamese light infantry battalions were activated for the effort and other Vietnamese battalions were formed into mobile groups to confront the Viet Minh regular formations. But this belated Vietnamization effort did not succeed militarily or politically. The enemy had grown too strong and the battle-tested Viet Minh regiments were too powerful for the weaker mobile groups to confront. And the crucial political ideal of nationalism in its amorphous state failed to galvanize the populace.

It was not until after the Geneva Accords were signed in 1954 that a new political consciousness was crystalized in the South with the establishment of the First Republic, and this political entity took its rightful place in the pacification planning and execution in South Vietnam.

---

[2] <u>People of the South, June 1952.</u> (A clandestine Communist monthly published in South Vietnam)

Strategy Under the First Republic of South Vietnam

The central characteristic of the South Vietnamese strategy was that it was defensive. This reflected the status of the South, born under difficult political circumstances after the 1954 Geneva Accords and whose national goal was nothing more than to build a free democracy with genuine sovereignty and protection from the aggressive designs of the Communists from the North. From a military point of view, North Vietnam, having trained, grown, and tested its forces and military commanders up to divisional level in the battles of the war of 1946-1954, had clear military superiority over the South.

The military threat from the North was envisaged by President Ngo Dinh Diem as appearing in two forms. The first was the threat of subversion created in the South by Communist military forces and Communist party members who stayed behind instead of going North as stipulated in the 1954 Geneva Accords. The second was the threat of invasion by regular North Vietnamese troops. To face this dual threat, the South's military strategy was designed to protect the territory against an invasion across its borders and to counter subversive activities within. The two key elements of the strategy called for (1) reorganizing the army to protect the frontiers and (2) gaining the support of the people through the Strategic Hamlets program. The task of defending national territory devolved mainly on the regular forces, aided by paramilitary forces. The regular forces were responsible for defending the borders against invasion and served as the general reserve; the paramilitary forces provided area defense, maintained law and order, and carried out pacification and anti-subversive operations.

After the 1954 Geneva Accords were signed the South Vietnamese Army had 205,000 men including 167,000 regulars and 38,000 in the auxiliary forces. The force was organized into 82 infantry battalions, 81 light infantry battalions, 5 airborne battalions, 6 Imperial Guard battalions, 9 artillery battalions, 4 engineer battalions, 6 transportation battalions, and 10 armored reconnaissance companies. Air support consisted of only one liaison flight and two combat support observation companies.

President Diem's military organization plan called for a force built around nine infantry divisions and one airborne division. This plan was submitted to the MAAG for discussion and funding. The MAAG would not approve the airborne division and would provide funding, from July 1955 on, for only four standard infantry divisions and six light divisions. Therefore, although President Diem would have the ten divisions he asked for, the force would lack the offensive capability found in an airborne division and it would also be less capable of sustained defense in conventional combat.

It was apparent that the Americans felt that four infantry divisions — called "field" divisions to distinguish them from the light divisions — would be sufficient to defend the frontiers against overt invasion. These field divisions were organized at a strength of 8,600 which was considerably smaller than a U.S. infantry division, but they contained their own administrative, logistic and combat support units, including one battalion of 105-mm howitzers, and were considered capable of independent, sustained combat.

The light divisions were organized for a different primary mission: that of operating against enemy insurgents in isolated, difficult terrain, employing, when appropriate, guerrilla tactics and techniques. They were to capitalize on their mobility in attacking enemy base areas and sanctuaries. They lacked the logistic and fire support of the field divisions and thus could deploy more rapidly. Their authorized strength was only 5,245 and their heaviest organic fire support were 81-mm mortars.

With this ten-division force as the core of the Army of the Republic of Vietnam (ARVN) other combat and combat support elements included an airborne brigade, four armored cavalry squadrons, and eleven separate light artillery battalions.

In 1955, two of the four field divisions were deployed to defend the northern frontier against an invasion across the Demilitarized Zone (DMZ). One was located in the Central Highlands to reinforce the defense of the invasion route at the tri-border. The fourth field division was positioned near Saigon as general reserve and to block the potential invasion route at the Tay Ninh Province border.

One of the six light divisions was stationed in the north to reinforce the two field divisions there. One was also in the Central Highlands in Kontum Province to help secure the tri-border area. Two other light divisions were deployed from the central coast along the major highways to the highlands. The remaining two divisions were in the Mekong Delta to protect the large population centers found there.

At the end of 1958 the Americans promoted the concept that the light divisions should be converted into field divisions. When this was done there were no longer units designed and equipped for quick forays into enemy sanctuaries and remote bases. Seeing this void President Diem authorized the formation of ranger units to take over this mission. Accordingly, in late 1962, every fourth company of every infantry battalion became the ranger company. There were 65 such companies and most of them received their special training in actual combat rather than in any training center. Officers and non-commissioned officers with extensive combat experience were encouraged to transfer to ranger companies. Later, when the enemy began to operate in battalions, the rangers — now with U.S. encouragement and support — were organized into twenty battalions, placed under the command of the military region commanders, and employed throughout the military regions rather than within the sectors as before.

Territorial forces, separate from the National Army, existed in Vietnam since 1948. By 1955 there were 13 territorial regiments throughout the country. Until the end of the war in 1954 they were known by different names depending on the governor they belonged to: North, Central or South Vietnam (Cochin). For example, in North Vietnam they were known as *Bao Chinh Doan*, which was an abbreviated way of saying "forces that defend the administration and the just nationalist cause." Because the *Bao Chinh Doan* were closely associated with the nationalist *Dai Viet* political party they were considered by the French to be the military forces of the *Dai Viets*. Since the *Dai Viets* had opposed the French in 1940, the French would have no part in supporting the *Bao Chinh Doan*.

In Central Vietnam the situation was quite different. The French supported Bao Dai and therefore the territorial force organized by Bao Dai loyalist Phan Van Giao in 1948. This force was called *Viet Binh Doan*

Vietnamese Rangers Boarding U.S. Army H-21 Helicopters
in an Operation Against Viet Cong Bases in the Plain of Reeds in 1962

Ranger Observation Post Near Trung Lap, May 1962

which simply meant Vietnamese Military Group. But the initials — VBD — were widely interpreted to mean "*Vi Bao Dai*" and "*Voi Bao Dai*;" in English, "for and with Bao Dai."

In the South the French supported the *Ve Binh Quoc Gia* — National Guard — and entrusted it with administrative functions as well as military security operations.

In April 1955, the territorial forces of Central and South Vietnam were unified under the title of Civil Guard (CG). The Civil Guard (CG) came under the jurisdiction of the Interior Ministry. Organized into squads, platoons, companies, and battalions, it was assigned the dual mission of maintaining law and order and participating in civic action programs. In practice the Ministry of Interior had only administrative control of the Civil Guard; the units were actually commanded by the Province Chiefs. While the CG operated at the provincial level, at the village level security was the responsibility of the Self-Defense units whose members were recruited from among villagers. They were equipped with rudimentary arms and had no uniforms.

As a consequence of the 1954 Geneva Accords, peace was restored and American policy provided that U.S. military assistance would support a South Vietnamese army of only 150,000 men. This remained the constant strength from June 1955 to August 1961. The Americans permitted it to increase only when the military threat from the North became all too obvious. Though constrained within the strength limit of 150,000 men, the First Republic's military planning demonstrated the South's concern about the military threat from the North, and provided for counter-measures as they were required by the situation.

First of all, new types of units were activated to bolster the defense of border and coastal areas and to achieve mobility and offset the weaknesses of an area type of defense. The first of these were the Vietnamese Special Forces, created in 1957 and patterned after the organization and modes of operation of the U.S. Army Special Forces. The soldiers in the special forces units were recruited from the ethnic groups and tribes in the highlands and swamps where the units operated. Not only were these soldiers familiar with the terrain and weather and therefore able to endure the hardships of life in the rugged frontier areas of South Vietnam, but employment of the highland tribes in particular countered the efforts of the Viet Cong who attempted to incite the tribal groups against the government and exploit the long-standing animosities between the tribes and the government.

Built along the Lao and Cambodian borders, special forces camps blocked avenues of approach leading into the First and Second Military Regions. Camps were also set up in unpopulated back country from which border patrols, trail surveillance, raids, and reconnaissance missions could be staged.

Maritime patrol units were activated in 1960 to reduce the amount of supplies and infiltrators being sent by sea from the North into the coasts of South Vietnam. Fishermen who were familiar with local shipping and fishing patterns and who knew the coastline and hiding places were recruited for these patrols. Meanwhile, the Vietnamese Navy patrolled farther out at sea and the Regional Forces (RF) and police maintained surveillance in the coastal villages. This three-sided operation—deep sea, coastal waters and ashore—was established from the 17th parallel in the north, around Cape Ca Mau, and to the Cambodian border at Ha Tien. The boats the coastal units used were of the type used by fishermen in the particular region. For example, in Quang Tri and Thua Thien they used the local woven-hulled sailing craft. Later an improved motorized junk was developed and built in the Vietnamese Navy shipyards. This craft, the Yabuta junk, was faster and more seaworthy than the traditional fishing boats and it was deployed throughout the system. By the end of 1961, the Vietnamese Navy was operating eight patrol boat groups, each with 20 boats.

Improving Communications and Control

When North Vietnam made plans to conquer the South in 1958, one of its major considerations was the introduction of men and weapons. Securing a safe infiltration route for this purpose was therefore a primordial task to be achieved above everything else. During the survey process, Hanoi's agents reconnoitered all access roads along the Laotian panhandle's

eastern area and the western border strip of upper South Vietnam. The
major task of putting this infiltration road system together and testing
its practicability was eventually assigned to a team led by an elderly
southern-born cadre who had reputed knowledge of local road communications.
This man made a long journey in the reverse direction, departing from
South Vietnam and consulting as he progressed north with local Viet Minh
agents to select the best practicable route. In time, this famous
infiltration route became known to the West as the Ho Chi Minh Trail, an
old name dating from the days of the First Indochina War. Many Communist
cadres, however, called it "The Old Man Trail" as a special tribute to
the man who had pioneered it.

While North Vietnam surveyed and prepared this infiltration route,
President Ngo Dinh Diem also decided to improve South Vietnam's road
system. His concern was primarily strategic. In his thinking, the road
network would have to be expanded to permit the rapid deployment of
fighting units to strike enemy bases, to defend threatened areas, and
to support ARVN units occupying remote outposts. Consequently, in 1958
he inaugurated the strategic highway improvement plan. In Military
Region 1, work was started on a link between Highway 1 and Nam Dong
via Bach Ma Pass and between Nam Dong and the A Shau Valley. This
would make it possible to resupply the outposts in the A Shau Valley
by vehicle rather than only by air. National Highway 9 was repaired
to link Dong Ha to Khe Sanh and Lao Bao, the gateway to the Lao border.

In Military Region 2, National Highway 19 was repaired and
enlarged at the An Khe and Mang Yang Passes to allow for better access
to the highlands of Pleiku from the coastal lowlands of Binh Dinh.
National Highway 14 was reconnoitered north of Kontum for the
feasibility of linkage between Military Region 2 and the seaport of
Danang. Sections of the countryside from Ban Me Thuot to Dalat and
from Di Linh to Phan Thiet were surveyed for road construction also.

In Military Region 3, the strategic Saigon-Bien Hoa highway was
built, slicing through the VC An Phu Dong base area and providing rapid
access to MR-3 headquarters and on QL-15 to Vung Tau.

Waterways were an integral part of the plan. In Military Region 4, the Dong Tien Canal was cut across the VC Dong Thap Muoi (Plain of Reeds) secret zone to link with the waterway systems of Military Regions 3 and 4.

A study of the provincial organization and boundaries revealed that anti-guerrilla operations were rarely undertaken in the border areas between provinces and coordination between adjacent provinces was poor. The Viet Cong recognized this weakness and exploited it by locating their bases and liaison routes in the boundary regions. President Diem decided to rectify this situation by creating new provinces and boundaries that would centralize the responsibility in the hands of a single province chief for operations against some of the most important Viet Cong installations.

In Military Region 1, Quang Tin Province was created out of parts of Quang Nam and Quang Ngai in order to provide for better operations against the VC Bong Hong secret zone.

Phu Bon Province in Military Region 2 was carved out of four provinces: Pleiku, Binh Dinh, Ban Me Thuot, and Phu Yen. Highway 7B ran through Phu Bon Province and provided one more link between the highlands (Highway 14) and the coast (Highway 1). By creating Phu Bon the responsibility for security of this route was centralized.

The vast forested region along the Cambodian border with Ban Me Thuot and Binh Long Province could not be adequately covered from the capitals of these two provinces. Infiltration of Communists across the border from Cambodia was occurring unchecked. To deal with this problem two new provinces, Quang Duc and Phuoc Long, were created.

North of Saigon in Military Region 3, where the provinces of Binh Duong, Bien Hoa and Long Khanh met, President Diem created the new province of Phuoc Thanh. This was done to facilitate better control over operations against the VC liaison routes between War Zones C and D that passed through this area, and better coordinate operations in the VC secret zones west of National Route 13, the Boi Loi woods, Ho Bo woods, and the Long Nguyen secret zone. (This was the only province created by President Diem that did not survive his demise; it was eliminated when the new government determined that it was unnecessary.)

Another new province was created in Military Region 3: Hau Nghia. This province was constructed from parts of Tay Ninh, Binh Duong and Long An in order to provide better security along the Cambodian border west of Saigon in the region of the Parrot's Beak and Ba Thu.

Moc Hoa District of Long An Province became a province in Military Region 4, Kien Tuong. It was created to provide better control of Communist infiltration from Svay Rieng Province of Cambodia in the area of the Elephant's Foot. Two other new provinces established in Military Region 4 were Kien Phong and Sa Dec. Together with Kien Tuong, these new provinces provided better coordination for operations against the VC's famous Dong Thap Muoi secret zone which they boasted was impregnable.

Finally, the rich rice-growing region of the lower Mekong Delta between the provinces of Kien Giang, An Xuyen, Can Tho and Ba Xuyen, where VC activities were very hard to control, became Chuong Thien Province.

This entire territorial reorganization resulted in positioning provincial centers in key areas where there was intense enemy activity. The results were greater government control of all resources, better defined areas of responsibility, more economical distribution of forces, and greater opportunities for commanders to conduct better surveillance of and operations against the enemy.

Strategic Hamlets

In conjunction with the concepts of the strategic highway network and territorial reorganization, a social problem with important economic and military aspects cried out for attention. South Vietnam had over 800,000 refugees who had moved south after the 1954 treaty and thousands of other destitute people from poverty-stricken Central Vietnam. All these people would have to be resettled and provided opportunities to become self-supporting. Influenced more by military than by humanitarian, political or economic considerations, the resettlement program, which located the people in areas of military significance such as along strategic highways and in defensive belts around cities, revealed that the leaders of the First Republic recognized that the population was a strategic resource in itself that could be used in the national defense effort, a concept which they developed until it became a national stretegy: the strategy of the Strategic Hamlets.

In seventeenth and eighteenth century Vietnam, the southward movement of the Vietnamese people followed a settlement pattern consisting of agricultural settlements and plantations. As time passed, these settled areas became autonomous administratively and politically and evolved customs and practices which took precedence over national law. This situation was reflected in the ancient popular saying: "The king's law yields to the village's rules." The concept of autonomous zones was seen at work in the Phat Diem diocese, Kim Son District, Ninh Binh Province in North Vietnam. When asked in 1941 to be advisor to the Ho Chi Minh government, Bishop Le Huu Tu, then in charge of the diocese, asked that the Phat Diem area be made autonomous and placed under his own governance. His request was granted by the Ho Chi Minh administration and the area surrounding the Phat Diem seminary was declared self-governing and off-limits to communist activities. The Phat Diem congregation gradually expanded their dominion over the entire district of Kim Son. This experience was repeated in 1950 when the Bui Chu diocese of Nam Dinh Province in North Vietnam became the second such district to gain self-government.

In order to meet the military threat from the Viet Minh, Catholic leaders organized defensive units called Popular Force Regiments. These units were nowhere near regimental size, but consisted of the youths of the villages being defended. The volunteers were grouped into platoons and armed with rudimentary weapons such as machetes and spears. Villages were fortified and accesses, except for carefully guarded main gates, were entirely sealed off. Notwithstanding their primitive armaments and cursory military training, villages in these autonomous zones were able to repel Viet Minh attacks, thanks to high esprit and the network of defenses which included trenches, mines and booby traps.

President Diem and his brother Ngo Dinh Nhu (especially the latter) were not only devout Catholics but scholars of history and political science. The historical pattern of early agricultural settlements and the evolution of the autonomous zones of Bui Chu and Phat Diem greatly influenced the strategic thinking of these leaders of the First Republic. The idea of agricultural development was put into effect in several places such as the Lao Bao Agricultural Settlement in Quang Tri Province at the gateway to the Lao border on National Highway 9; the Nam Dong Settlement south of the city of Hue; the Hau Nghia Settlement adjacent to the Cambodian border near the Parrot's Beak and Ba Thu; the Tri Phap Settlement in the Dong Thap Muoi (Plain of Reeds) area, a famous Viet Minh sanctuary from 1945 to 1954. The locations of these settlements were dictated more by military considerations than by economic ones. This bias was redressed in July 1959 when the agricultural development program gave way to the Agroville program. Agrovilles were conceived with two objectives in mind: first, to create conditions favorable to economic and social development in rural areas; and second, to contribute to the maintenance of local security.

As a rule, agrovilles were built in areas formerly controlled by the enemy and along main arteries of communication in order to form secure corridors for the flow of traffic and commerce and for rescue missions to arrive from other areas. As incentives to encourage people to settle in agrovilles and to facilitate economic and social development, electricity and water, health and educational facilities and marketplaces were provided by the government. The expenses were paid partly out of the national budget and partly out of local taxes. A total of 23 agrovilles were built in 11 provinces, involving 32,000 people and 6,000 hectares of land strung along highways connecting cities such as Saigon, Dalat, Hue, and Danang.

The agroville program was flawed in that it created a completely new basic administrative unit. The people, raised in and accustomed to the hamlet as the basic social and administrative unit, had difficulty identifying with the agroville. Further, because each agroville assembled a large population of three to four thousand in a comparatively large area, defense and internal control became extremely difficult and were thus neglected.

With the demise of the agroville program in 1961, another idea went through a test in various localities and was finally proclaimed as a national policy in March 1962: the Strategic Hamlets. Hamlets were called strategic because they were the basic administrative units of the country and the very foundation of the program. They were to be built on a plan whose objective was to make changes in four areas: defense, politics, economics and social.

It was Counselor Nhu's theory that the villages of South Vietnam could be defended against VC armed forays if the hamlets were properly defended. It followed that if the defenses were properly designed and executed, all populated regions of the country would be secure. His concept for hamlet security was therefore crucial to the strategy. Although the concept was simple in design, it was difficult to execute, for it meant that a vast network of small but mutually supporting defensive positions would have to be constructed and manned throughout the populated countryside. This network, in theory, would provide for detection of all enemy movement in the zone and for effective mutual defense among the several hamlets of the villages. It would nullify the enemy's people's war strategy in this war that had no front line.

With regard to politics, each hamlet would institute democratic processes such as electing village councils and drafting the village charter and ordinances.

Economically, greater productivity would be achieved through planting new seeds. Guidance in new farming and animal husbandry techniques were provided by the government's agricultural experts.

For years the laws and rules that governed all aspects of life in the rural communities had been created by the village councils. Because membership on the village councils was the exclusive prerogative of wealthy land-owners, the laws and rules favored these men to the absolute exclusion of the peasants. Extreme abuses and cruelties were the result; physical punishment, for example, was not uncommonly administered for such an offense as non-payment of debt. Exhorbitant interest was charged on loans and the peasant's share of the rice crop was very small. The social structure of the Strategic Hamlets would change all this because the people would elect their own councils from among all villagers. The monopoly of the wealthy landlord would be broken.

Therefore, although the Strategic Hamlet program primarily sought military security it also sought to achieve political, economic, and social reforms. it was based on the premise that only when the masses begin to be concerned about their economic rights, their property rights, their political rights, their social privileges and the conveniences they are enjoying, will they wholeheartedly safeguard what they have and what they hold dear. In other words, the Strategic Hamlet plan strove to motivate the people to defend themselves and their families and to contribute to the defense of the community at large.

President Diem and Counselor Nhu exploited their understanding of the people's spirit and awareness of their public responsibilities to promote the Strategic Hamlets. In order to succeed, the people had to accept the idea of self-reliance in private as well as social life; of non-reliance on outside assistance. For example, the government initially loaned weapons to the people, usually 30 to each hamlet. Six months later each hamlet was to procure its own arsenal by capturing enemy weapons; the government would provide only ammunition. Hamlet defense barriers made use of locally available materials such as bamboo and thorn plants such as cacti and pineapple.

The Strategic Hamlet program created quite a sensation in the country. Intent on pushing the program to completion, the government required all civil servants, ranking civilian officials and military leaders to study the program. Local authorities, expected to prove to the central government their accomplishments in the program, spared no means to score high and in doing so alienated the people. For example, villages usually sprawl along waterways in the lowlands or along highways and pathways in the highlands. Attempts to gather the people into a centralized location was tantamount to placing them in a concentration camp of sorts. This forced relocation aggravated the people's discontent and grievances. Even before any tangible benefits had accrued, extensive material and morale damage was done. Villagers were forced to leave their homesteads for resettlement on new land and although they received some cash and building materials, these proved inadequate for erecting even temporary houses. The forced abandonment of old homes with their sacrosanct memories, gardens, lands, and ancestral graves were irreplaceable losses.

Forcible methods ran counter to the idea of voluntary participation of the Strategic Hamlet policy. President Diem was correct when he referred to the state of mind of the people as being vital to pacification, but he failed to understand that state of mind. The obligatory and excessive contributions of labor for such works as digging trenches and moats, and of cash to meet the operational costs of the hamlets, all exacted from villagers, were reminiscent of the forced labor and taxation system of French rule. These popular grievances added grist to the mill of opposition parties who protested against the policies of the authorities. The Communists exploited the feeling against the Strategic Hamlets not only by attacking them militarily but by waging a virulent propaganda campaign against them, demanding their elimination.

This violent opposition, however, was also an indication of the difficulty the Strategic Hamlet program had caused the VC. To a certain extent the strategy succeeded in separating the Communists from the masses and in denying them sources of food as well as other human, material, and financial resources. More important was the regrouping of the populace to the Nationalist side, its organization into people's groups, and its cooperation with the Nationalist government, which, though initially obtained through coercion, gradually became habitual.

The Revolution of 1 November 1963 toppled the First Republic. Immediately after the coup, Lieutenant General Ton That Dinh, the Minister of Interior for the new government, declared to newsmen that the Strategic Hamlet program of the House of Ngo had to be abolished. This statement was later denied by other members of the Revolutionary Committee, but a large number of Strategic Hamlets were dismantled by the Communists who took advantage of the troubled situation. Nevertheless, the Strategic Hamlet program was regarded by all subsequent governments as having strategic value, and with certain improvements and American aid, the South still considered pacification and rural development as the basis of a grand national strategy.

Watchtower Under Construction in a Strategic Hamlet, 1962

Women of the Civil Guard at Hoa Cam.
To the Rear, a Company of Men of the Civil Guard,
in the Summer of 1962

Women in the Local Militia in Military Drill, 1962

CHAPTER III

Strategy During the Period of U.S. Participation

The demise of the First Republic was followed by a period of political instability. This political instability eroded military security because high-ranking military leaders were more preoccupied with internal fighting. Communist strength grew apace and there were indications that the Third Strategic Stage, a general offensive, was imminent.

Indeed, in their estimate, Hanoi's leaders believed at this juncture that their military gains during 1964, coupled with an unprecedented political opportunity, were paving the way for ultimate success. But to wage a general offensive, their military forces in South Vietnam naturally needed to be augmented. As the first step, therefore, Hanoi deployed the 325th NVA Division to the Central Highlands with the determination to hold it. Pleiku and Kontum, the two major communication hubs of this area had always been our enemy's traditional objectives.

The strategic value of the Central Highlands, to our enemy, was clearly one of military geography. This important area lay adjacent to the last leg of the Laotian infiltration route which led into a bridgehead zone called the "Tri-Border" area. Joined with the Boloven Plateau further south, it offered an excellent platform from which avenues of approach could be carved into Cambodia and South Vietnam's MR-2 and MR-3. From the highland city of Pleiku toward the Binh Dinh coastal area, severing South Vietnam into two isolated halves along Route QL-19 would not be much of a difficulty, militarily speaking, provided that enough forces were available. The terrain of the Central Highlands also lent itself to enemy military activities because it provided concealment for troop movements, reduced the effect of air and artillery firepower and curtailed the use of armor by friendly forces.

The injection of U.S. military forces managed to relieve Communist pressure and save the South from immediate danger. During the first phase of American intervention, from 1965 to 1969, the American forces assumed the responsibility of destroying the enemy's main force, base areas and supply lines, defending border areas and the area below the demarcation line to interdict enemy infiltration from the North. The RVNAF responsibility was to commit its main effort to pacification and the development of populated areas. The coordinated action of the two armed forces, to destroy the enemy main force by military operations and to pacify the territory, caused the North Vietnamese to alter their strategy and attack the cities of the South in the offensive of 1968. Though a military defeat for the North this offensive scored a political victory, in that American political leaders became convinced that there would be no military victory for South Vietnam and that the war would drag on for years. This was the genesis of a new program of Vietnamization to expand and modernize the RVNAF and gradually to turn over all operational responsibilities to the Vietnamese as U.S. forces withdrew.

The South's strategy during the period of participation by American forces in the Vietnam war, from March 1965 to 27 January 1973, could be encapsulated in three main tasks: (1) continue the effort of pacification and rural development; (2) dismantle the enemy infrastructure through *Operation Phoenix*; and (3) expand and modernize the armed forces in accordance with *Vietnamization*.

Pacification and Rural Development

The Strategic Hamlet program of the First Republic, though severely criticized, was regarded by succeeding leaders of the South as the basic strategy to counter the North's plan to take over South Vietnam. Modifications in the techniques of execution were required, however, to correct weaknesses and to profit by the experiences of the First Republic. The Plan for Victory (*Chien Thang*) made official in March 1964, required some modifications, the first of which was renaming Strategic Hamlets; they became New Life hamlets.

The Victory Plan was based on the oil slick principle, implementing pacification first in heavily populated and prosperous areas, and gradually spreading to less populated and less prosperous ones. Capitalizing on the criticims of the Strategic Hamlet program, the Victory Plan introduced a number of other modifications such as reducing excessive resettlements, compensating the people for damages incurred by resettlement, avoiding unnecessary planting of mines and booby traps, avoiding press-ganging the people into projects that were the government's responsibility such as road building and ditch digging.

The Victory Plan still exhibited serious weaknesses, however. There was a lack of coordination between the civilian and military agencies. Secondly, funds earmarked for resettlement damage compensation and construction of public utilities were inadequate. Thirdly, there was a shortage of qualified government officials at the local level to supervise the program.

In the beginning, the RVNAF were not yet organized or equipped to provide the support the New Life Hamlet program needed. A typical example of their limitation was their response to rescue and defense mission requests from New Life hamlets. The hamlet defense forces had the capability to discover impending enemy attacks and to offer brief resistance after the attacks began. They needed help from the ARVN to survive determined enemy attacks. The best night support available for them was artillery firepower, and yet there was no direct communication link between hamlets under attack and artillery units.

Until the mission of the RVNAF was clearly defined as being primarily pacification, RVNAF had to split its resources between military operations and pacification support. In 1965 this mission was defined as pacification support but it was not until 1966 that the RVNAF was really ready to assume the mission. Units had to be trained in the pacification effort, in civic action and in techniques to gain the support of the people.

The size and category of the armed forces to be employed in a particular pacification mission depended on the status of security in each locality. Four classifications of security were defined to provide the basis for this judgement. An area was considered secure where local government could function normally without threat from enemy forces, although terrorist action and sporadic shelling might occur. Law and order in secure areas were maintained by National Police with the support of Popular Forces and Self-Defense Forces. The responsibility of the Regional Forces was to conduct security patrols in adjoining areas in order to prevent enemy encroachment into the secure area.

The consolidation area was the next category. In this area there was no threat from large enemy units but terrorist activities and shellings were more frequent and curfew had to be imposed. Consolidation areas were considered security belts, buffers around secure areas. Regional Forces were the key forces operating in consolidation areas, supported and reinforced by Popular Forces (PF), National Police (NP) and Self-Defense Forces. The support of infantry divisions was available when needed.

A mop-up area was sparsely populated and largely controlled by the Communists. Every action by the RVNAF in this area was against Communist main forces and their base areas to prevent them from infiltrating consolidation areas. Mop-up areas were under the control of infantry division commanders or commanding officers of tactical units, with support provided, when necessary, by U.S. and Free World Forces.

The last category was the border defense area. Military region and corps commanders were responsible for detecting and preventing enemy invasions of Vietnamese territory through the border area, but the defense of the area was conducted by border defense forces supported, when necessary, by U.S. forces.

In order for pacification (revolutionary development) plans and military plans to mesh, plans drawn up by province chiefs had to be reviewed and approved by division and corps commanders prior to being submitted to the Ministry of Rural Development. This approval was necessary to show that the divisions and corps had the capability of supporting the pacification effort in the area concerned.

The mission of the RVNAF, in their supporting role *vis-à-vis* the pacification and rural development consisted of conducting mopping-up operations of areas chosen for pacification; establishing, improving, and maintaining security in those areas at a high level until the re-

Regular ARVN Infantrymen of the 1st Battalion, 33d Infantry, 21st Division During an Operation in the Mekong Delta, An Xuyen Province, 1967

volutionary development project had been achieved; and at the same time, protecting developed areas against relapsing into enemy control.

From 1969 on, as the RVNAF gradually regained operational responsibilities, Regional Forces and Popular Forces replaced regular infantry battalions and infantry divisions would reinforce RF and PF only on order from division tactical zone commanders and in vital areas which RF and PF were incapable of handling. Thus the principal forces that supported the pacification effort were Regional and Popular Forces. RF units provided mobile defense in the areas lying between hamlets and villages, along enemy routes of communication and set up a distant security belt for PF units. The main objective of RF were VC provincial guerrilla units. PF units served in their own village or hamlet, protected the people, the resources and fixed installations. PF operated in the hamlets and not far away from them; their main targets were local guerrilla units.

Compared with the pacification effort of the years 1962 to 1967, the pacification and rural development effort of the years after 1967 registered marked improvements on several fronts. In terms of commitment, greater determination was evident in the utilization of regular forces, thus avoiding the criticism that military operations had no connection with pacification. There were adequate funds to finance government projects aimed at achieving economic and social goals. The government created the Ministry of Rural Development to coordinate operations of all ministries having rural projects while the American side set up a unified agency called Civil Operations and Revolutionary Development Support (CORDS) to take charge of pacification.

An annual combined military plan called Plan AB was developed by the Joint General Staff and the Military Assistance Command, Vietnam (MACV). It spelled out missions and tasks for the RVNAF and U.S. forces and Free World Forces in support of pacification and rural development. Serious weaknesses appeared in the plan, however. One was the selection of priority objectives within areas under pacification. Priority objectives were assigned at the provincial level. Priorities were dictated by the security situation, the need for support, the progress of programs, local capabilities, and so on. Though reasonable in principle this resulted in 44 priority target areas in as many provinces, and no overall priority areas on the national or military region level. The organizational principle of national planning which calls for priorities to be established at the highest level, priorities that correlate to the national strategy, had been reversed. The result was that no two plans for adjacent provinces were mutually compatible and provincial border areas were ignored. The Communists, capitalizing on the neglect, set up their base areas in these border regions. Each province and district chief looked to the neighboring jurisdiction to handle the problem but few did.

Another weakness lay in the fact that local authorities frequently selected priority target areas that would lend themselves to easy success so that favorable reports might later be filed with the Central Development Council and favorable evaluations would be made by inspectors.

Another weakness resided in the fact that infantry battalions and regiments were assigned to sector commands in support of the pacification and rural development effort. This meant that division commanders were unable to control their units and divisional staffs had few opportunities to plan operations at the divisional level. Moreover, battalions and regiments assigned to local military authorities were further split into company-size units so that ultimately it was only at the company level that action was actually performed and experience gained. A serious command and control problem was the result. Although the division commander relinquished control of battalions to sector commanders, the sector commanders actually assumed little control. The battalions still reported to and received orders from their regiments and all activities and operations by the battalions in support of pacification depended on cooperation and such good will that the sector commander could achieve with the battalion commander.

Generally speaking, the commitment of divisional units to the support of rural development, though it increased the capabilities and resources available for the effort, resulted in a decrease in the fighting competence and ability of the units. Furthermore, as time went by, these units slowly acquired the complacency of stationary forces more accustomed to area defense than to offensive operations. It was easier to introduce an infantry unit into an area than to remove it. The people, accustomed to the presence of regular units, felt their confidence shaken when these units were withdrawn because they lacked faith in the RF and PF. Morale among the RF and PF also suffered when regular units departed. They knew that their security had been diminished and that the VC were likely to exploit this weakness.

But the most important weakness in the pacification strategy was, up to this point, not even recognized. This was the fact that no concerted action was being taken to destroy the Viet Cong Infrastructure (VCI), that complex, widespread apparatus that provided essential support to the military arm of the Viet Cong and directed the entire insurgency effort.

It was true that the government of the First Republic had correctly regarded the VCI as a dangerous force to contend with. As early as 1958, therefore, efforts to eliminate it were carried out in secret under orders from the Independence Palace. President Diem's campaign against the VCI was effective but indiscriminate. By authorizing province chiefs to execute suspects without a hearing or even a police record, he in effect encouraged abuses. There is little doubt that many political enemies—who were not actually VC—disappeared as a result of the anti-VCI campaign. In any event, Mr. Diem's efforts ended with his overthrow in late 1963.

The successive South Vietnamese governments after him were too beset by power struggle to take any interest in combating the VCI. Lacking direction and guidance, no GVN organization took this task seriously or was equipped to monitor and take action against it.

The Armed Forces believed that they had no responsibility for action against the VCI; that was the exclusive responsibility of the National Police. The National Police meanwhile were undermanned for the task and ineffective. Therefore, despite suffering heavy losses on the battlefields, the enemy continued his terror and sabotage campaign right in the Saigon metropolitan area, collected taxes, recruited personnel, and gathered supplies under the very noses of the police.

Not until 1967 was the vital role of the enemy infrastructure perceived as the political and administrative arms of the Viet Cong.

Its vital missions were to provide support to VC military forces by supplying them with money, food, equipment, medicines, manpower, and services; to prepare for the eventual takeover of the government by securing the allegiance of the people of the South; and to prepare a cadre capable of playing leading roles in a future coalition government.

The importance of the enemy infrastructure was finally realized by the U.S. The plan to eliminate the enemy infrastructure, proposed by the U.S. and approved by the Vietnam government, was put into effect in 1967 and made public under the appellation of *Operation Phoenix* in August of 1968.

Operation Phoenix

The enemy infrastructure was organized from the central level to the rice-roots level and existed in three important organizations: the Central Office for the South (COSVN), the National Front for the Liberation of the South (NLF), and the People's Revolutionary Party (PRP).

In areas under Communist control, the Viet Cong infrastructure controlled the population, collected taxes, impressed the people to work and farm, operated people's courts, and drafted the people into military service. In contested areas the enemy infrastructure disrupted the government's rural programs, conducted assassinations, kidnapped hamlet and village officers, collected taxes with the aid and support of armed guerrilla bands, sabotaged routes of communication, conducted financial, economic and trade operations to supply its armed forces, carried on propaganda activities, and operated a communications and liaison system. In areas under government control, the underground's operations were entirely covert and assumed both legal and illegal aspects. Agents were legal when they lived in government-controlled areas, had legal identification papers, and held ordinary jobs which were used as cover for their activities. Illegal agents had no legal residence, were not on the family census cards, had no legal identification papers and no employment.

The operations of the VCI included terrorist and sabotage activities; covert propaganda activities; purchase of important supplies such as medical and pharmaceutical products and controlled merchandise such as power generators, outboard motors, FM radios and so on; sheltering cadres on temporary assignments from outside city limits; storing documents, weapons and explosives; and supplying intelligence information. In short, the VCI operated as a *de facto* government in areas under its control and guided VC operations in contested and government-controlled areas. In concert with armed guerrillas, regional forces and special mission units when needed, VCI was an important and effective force in the war of insurgency and sabotage. Its operations gave the impression of communist omnipresence and versatility, eroding the people's faith in the government.

The strength of the VCI was estimated at 80 to 90 thousand just before the *Tet* Offensive of 1968. During this offensive, the covert personnel were assigned the mission of surfacing to fight in the cities, attacking military targets, serving as guides to enemy troops, inciting the people to revolt, and supplying Communist military units. As a result of this emergence from cover, as many as half of the VCI personnel were killed.

Were it not for their exposure during this offensive, members of the VCI would have been difficult to flush out and destroy in any significant numbers. Unlike the Communists' armed units which had names, designations, habitual areas of operation, recognizable fighting methods, and whose activities could be detected through different sources of information, VCI was hard to identify because of the small size (three to ten persons) of its cells, its dispersion and immersion in the population, and its clandestine and irregular activities.

When MACV began planning a program to combat the VCI in 1967, the planners realized that gathering intelligence was one of the first tasks to be accomplished. After that, forces had to be available to deal with the VCI units and members uncovered. It was therefore obvious that close coordination between civilian and military intelligence agencies and between the police and military units had to be developed. It was out of this concept of coordination—*phoi hop* in Vietnamese—that the name for the operation was derived. The initial letters of *phoi hop* could also stand for *Phuong Hoang* which was the name of the mythical "King of the Chickens" who lived in the deep forests and devoured millipedes. The VCI was lined to the millipede and the *Phuong Hoang* would devour the VCI. The Americans understood that the Vietnamese had named the operation after a powerful bird, but since western mythology didn't have a "King of the Chickens," the immortal *Phoenix* was substituted.

The *Phoenix Program* was organized from the national down to the district level. The operating agencies at the provincial level were Provincial Intelligence Operations Coordination Committees (IOCC); those of the district level, District Intelligence Operations Coordination Committees.

Conceived as a long-range program, *Operation Phoenix* was to be executed both in war and peace and the National Police were responsible for its execution. At all levels, military and civilian intelligence agencies cooperated closely in gathering, comparing and evaluating information on the enemy infrastructure, and in supplying objectives for military operations.

Missions against the infrastructure could be conducted as combined operations under the command of Coordination Committees acting in conjunction with RVNAF or allied forces, or as unilateral operations. Combined operaions normally occurred when there were search-and-destroy operations, pacification operations, and operations against the infrastructure occurring in the same area at the same time. In such situations the armed forces would provide logistical support such as transportation and security against Communist military reaction by setting up security belts on the perimeter. RF and PF units would have the mission of encircling objective areas, protecting police search-and-screen teams and establishing combined tactical screening centers.

At the provincial and district levels, police chiefs, in their capacity as Second Vice Chairmen of the IOCC, directed the ARVN S-2's and S-3's who were heads of the situation section and the operations section respectively.

The operational forces organic to the National Police were the Field Police Forces. These forces conducted encirclement, raid and ambush operations on targets which the Special Police division of the National Police had planned and defined. The Field Police had a further mission to prevent the enemy underground or guerrillas from resuming their activities in areas which had been brought under control and to assure protection as the National Police developed in the countryside.

From March 1969, the police operational forces were joined by Provincial Reconnaissance Units (PRU). These were organized, recruited, and trained by an element of the United States CIA organization. The mission of the Provincial Reconnaissance Units was to plan and participate in destroy operations, to participate in operations planned by PIOCCs and DIOCCs to assist RVNAF and allied forces in reconnoitering and determining objectives, and to gather information on the VCI. Provincial Reconnaissance Unit personnel, who were recruited from among ARVN veterans and VC defectors, received special training by CIA agents at the PRU Training Center in Vung Tau. The local security situation dictated the number of PRUs assigned to each province. Before their transfer to the National Police, the PRUs were controlled directly by the American adviser assigned to the province for that specific purpose.

As a rule, PRUs were effective and aggressive, thanks to their thorough training, excellent armament and higher pay as compared with the pay of soldiers in the RVNAF. However, this proved to be a weakness of the PRU. Because of their mercenary nature (controlled by Americans) and the absence of a Vietnamese character, there arose a lack of harmony between PRUs on the one hand, and the RVNAF units and the populace on the other. This was probably the reason for placing PRUs under the overall control of the Directorate of National Police, and under the operational control of province chiefs in 1969. Finally, in order to eliminate the enduring problems of control, the PRUs were integrated with the Field Police in 1970.

To provide for involvement by the RVNAF, military region commanders were given the responsibility of carrying out *Phoenix* within their jurisdictions. Elevated to the nation's strategic policy level, the program to eliminate the VCI enjoyed the financial and material backing of CORDS and MACV and produced impressive results. Like so many others however, this program was flawed by a number of deficiencies, among them some incorrigible cadre.

From the point of view of logical organization, assigning the main responsibility of eliminating the VCI to the National Police made sense, but in practice the National Police lacked the capability to discharge the responsibility. At the time it took on this project, the National Police had only 66,000 men and no organization at the district level, although by 1972 the Police strength reached 120,000. Inevitably, this rapid expansion was possible only by lowering standards of training and experience and there was a perennial shortage of qualified leaders. Province police chiefs were only second lieutenants; and at the district level the ranking police official was a noncommissioned officer. For the most part, they were freshly graduated from the Police Academy and lacked specialized knowledge and experience. Yet in the administration of the *Phoenix Program* they were supposed to direct the activities of ARVN officers, usually experienced captains who were province intelligence and operations officers. Even at the district level the police officer was out-ranked by the ARVN intelligence and operations officers. The result was that the police official had very little influence over policy or operations. Because of his low rank and lack of experience, the province or district police official, even though he was vice chairman of the IOCC, could not issue instructions regarding intelligence or operations to the military staffs because the province or district chief, who was an ARVN officer, reserved this right for himself. Representatives from other agencies on the PIOCC and DIOCC were in the same situation, and generally speaking, were no more competent than the police official at those levels.

Phoenix was never effective at the district level and was an absolute failure as a village-level operation. The reason was that there were not enough qualified people to deploy to the districts and villages to run the program. Nevertheless, the VCI lost a lot of members during 1968 and 1969 through the combination of its disastrous experience during the 1968 offensive and effective *Phoenix* operations in the provinces.

One of the most difficult issues that arose during the campaign against the VCI involved the treatment of suspects captured. The status of each captured person was decided by the provincial security committee headed by province chiefs; the captive could be either released or held for trial depending on the evidence presented at the committee hearing. The large number of VCI members detained for trial caused congestion at the courts, which convened only once a month. Trials were far from fair because they were conducted in haste and because witnesses gave secret testimony. In 1971, even after the central government ordered trials to take place at least once a week, local conditions did not permit speedy or fair trials. Consequently, long detention and unfair trials gave rise to considerable popular grievances, resentments, and opposition by families of suspects. There is no doubt that many suspects were victims of circumstance rather than committed and active enemies of the state.

Another weakness lay in the fact that military unit commanders felt little enthusiasm to launch operations against an enemy that was not an armed unit but lived, from outward appearances, like all law-abiding citizens. They felt that this unarmed enemy was not their proper adversary; he was the responsibility of the National Police. Military officers doing administrative duties such as province chiefs and district chiefs were, however, fully convinced of the threat posed by the VCI and zealously executed *Phoenix*.

In 1970, the chief of Quang Tin Sector had an original idea and named the operation against the infrastructure the Simultaneous Offensive Campaign. According to plan, on a secretly predetermined day all paramilitary forces, National Police, Revolutionary Development teams, armed propaganda teams, Open Arms, and Self-Defense Forces acting in conjunction with RF and PF would launch a concerted offensive against all VCI targets in the area. Certain RF units, guided by defectors, would stage raids on sanctuary areas of VC district and village commissars. Objectives selected by local forces tended to be the most productive because of the accurate and detailed knowledge the locals usually had concerning the local VCI.

The first Simultaneous Offensive operation launched in Quang Tin lasted three days and resulted in about 200 members of the VCI and guerrillas killed or captured. These unprecedented results were achieved through concerted action and the resulting confusion into which the enemy was thrown, making it impossible for him to find shelter.

Simultaneous Offensive operations were later duplicated by other provinces and eventually by military regions. By the end of 1970 the Fourth Military Region had carried out Simultaneous Offensive operations throughout its territory with the participation of Vietnamese infantry divisions. In the first such operation between 300 and 500 VCI members and guerrillas were eliminated.

Following early spectacular success, the effectiveness of Simultaneous Offensive operations diminished gradually. This was because the VCI was being eliminated and lucrative targets no longer existed. Furthermore, those elements of the VCI that remained adopted extreme measures to protect themselves. Enemy cadres became much more cautious and reduced their activities. Meanwhile the Self-Defense elements in the villages that had participated so effectively in these operations enjoyed new recognition and heightened morale.

When the Communists launched their Summer 1972 General Offensive, the role of the underground was, if not eclipsed, no longer nearly as prominent as it had been during the 1968 *Tet* offensive. But *Phoenix* came under attack by the American press and peace activists to the point that it had to be terminated.

Vietnamization

The enemy's 1968 offensive, although a Communist military failure, resulted in a significant change in U.S. policy toward the war.[1] A reflection of this change was contained in U.S. Defense Secretary Clifford's statement of 8 April 1968 to the effect that the main responsibility for prosecuting the war would be gradually handed over to the Republic of Vietnam. This policy took shape in the *Vietnamization* program announced at the Midway Conference on 8 June. The objectives

---

[1] For more detail concerning enemy strategy during the 1968-69 offensives, see Chapter II of the General Offensives of 1968-69 by the same author.

Vietnamization: 105-mm Howitzers
of the 9th U.S. Infantry Division are Turned Over to
the ARVN 213th Artillery Battalion at Can Tho, 26 April 1969

of *Vietnamization* were outlined by Defense Secretary Melvin R. Laid as follows:

- To turn over military responsibility to the South by giving it sufficient strength to withstand invasion.
- To reduce American losses.
- To maintain U.S. obligations and interests in Asia while heading toward peace.

Vietnamization was to be accomplished in three phases:

Phase 1: Turn over to the South the responsibility of land operations againt Communist forces.

Phase 2: Expand the South's military strength in air, naval and artillery power, in logistics and in other supporting capabilities necessary to insure national security.

Phase 3: Reduce American presence to the role of military adviser, and maintain a small force in defense of this role until the South reaches full growth and self-sufficiency and no longer requires U.S. military presence.

The government of Vietnam presented the U.S. with three proposals at the Midway Conference: (1) to expand the RVNAF: (2) to push vigorously the modernization of the RVNAF; and (3) to increase aid in raising the standard of living of the RVNAF and their families.

The program to expand the RVNAF resulted in an increase of authorized strength from 712,214 at the end of 1968 to 1,045,500 in fiscal year 1970, and to 1,100,000 in fiscal year 1973. This raised the troop strength to a percentage of the population considered by the government to be appropriate. This percentage was 6.5%, and if all armed civil defense forces were counted, amounted to 13%. (Applied to the population of the United States a percentage of 6.5% would have provided a U.S. military force of 13 million men.) The Army had ten infantry divisions and two general reserve divisions of marines and paratroopers. In 1973 the Navy's strength increased to 40,000 men, and that of the Air Force to 60,000 men.

With the contemplated strength of 1.1 million men, which the United States had agreed to equip, the GVN planned a powerful military establishment equipped with modern weapons. This planning was motivated by two factors. The first was the fact that during the period of American participation in the war, the RVNAF had become accustomed to and impressed by the organization of the U.S. armed forces and their tremendous firepower and mobility. The ideal to which the RVNAF aspired was nothing less than the kind of equipment and tactics U.S. forces employed.

Secondly, there were increasing indications that Communist forces were moving towards a conventional type of warfare. Their units were gradually organized into division; their combat arms were fighting with newer weapons, tanks, heavy artillery, rockets, and communications. Therefore RVNAF had to be equipped with weapons at least as modern as those the Communists were employing.

Priority was given to activating additional divisions to replace eight allied divisions—six American and two Korean—which would eventually leave. The creation of new divisions was initially opposed by MACV and for a while RVNAF increased its strength by adding a fourth unit at each echelon so that regiments had four battalions and battalions had four companies.

To share in the operational responsibility which RVNAF assumed as a result of Vietnamization, RF and PF took on the tasks of pacification and revolutionary development in addition to their territorial security mission. Somewhat paradoxically, the more progress that was made in pacification and revolutionary development—that is, as more hamlets were made secure—the greater became the requirements for forces to protect the gains made. Inevitably RVNAF were spread thin over the countryside to prevent enemy units from reentering and nullifying the success. Furthermore, the threat increased as the enemy developed more better equipped and well trained sapper units whose prime targets were important industrial and military installations. This meant that many RF and PF units were occupied protecting power plants, water and irrigation systems, warehouses, cement plants, and sugar and rice mills.

Sentry Post Manned by a Popular Forces Unit
Guarding a Bridge Over a Canal, 1970

A rundown of RF and PF missions for the second half of 1969, after the Vietnamization process had begun, was as follows:

RF Missions	Units Involved
Hamlet and village security	391
District and provincial security	207
Guarding important facilities	116
Highway security	211
Offensive operations	215

PF Missions	Units Involved
Hamlet and village security	3,184
District and provincial security	552
Guarding important facilities	112
Highway security	591
Offensive operations	100

As can be seen, 19 percent of RF and 2 percent of PF were engaged in offensive operations. These percentages could be increased only at the expense of security duties. It was obvious that if the missions assigned to the RF and PF could not be appreciably reduced, we should take some steps to improve the efficiency with which the units operated.

In 1970 the territorial forces were finally integrated into the RVNAF; no longer were they considered paramilitary. Improvements in the combat capabilities of the territorials—some generated by American interest and assistance such as coordination in operations with regular U.S. forces and special programs such as the U.S. Marine Corps Combined Action Team Program (CAT) in I Corps—were apparent as early as 1967. In 1968 the territorials were thrown into heavy combat against regular NVA formations. Determined to defend their villages at all costs, many territorial units fought extremely well, repelled the enemy, and in doing so gained a measure of new confidence and pride. Although the territorial officers and soldiers knew that they had performed well, their morale suffered from a lack of government recognition. The integration of 1970 helped ameliorate this problem.

The Long An territorials, deployed during the invasion of Cambodia in 1970, secured lines of communication and performed so well in battle that they surprised regular troops as well as themselves. The RF were now able to use stronger support such as helicopter transportation and artillery firepower from Vietnamese and U.S. units. A major problem, however, remained that of coordination; there was no direct communication between supporting and supported units. RF and PF had to go through the sector and subsector communication channels. Consequently, in case of enemy attack, in some particular cases it could take as long as 45 minutes for friendly supporting fire and as many as 24 hours for reinforcements to arrive.

Before Vietnamization, the RF's areas of operation were confined to provincial boundaries but from 1969 onward they were organized into company groups and battalions and there were instances where they were employed outside their home provinces.

Until their reorganization in 1970, PF served only part-time and were paid accordingly; they held regualr daytime jobs. Their armaments consisted of rejects from regular forces: shotguns, bolt-action French rifles, carbines and M-1 rifles. In any project involving the armed forces, the PF had last priority.

The basic unit of PF was the platoon, and its area of activities, the hamlet. Two important missions which these platoons could perform were intelligence collection and psywar. One characteristic of PF was their ability to maintain a close relationship with the local populace far more easily than either regular forces or RF could. Properly exploited, this close rapport enjoyed by PF should have made them a link between the armed forces and the masses, and would have greatly facilitated the task of winning the people's hearts and minds. Unfortunately, no one made any significant effort in this direction.

There were about 12,000 hamlets in the country. With over 8,300 PF platoons and more than 1,600 RF companies, a rough average existed of one PF platoon or RF company for each hamlet.

The need for modernization of the entire RVNAF—not only the territorial forces—was recognized by South Vietnamese military leaders long before the Americans announced *Vietnamization*. In 1965, the RVNAF with an antiquated collection of diverse weapons, were fighting regular NVA infantry regiments equipped with modern automatic weapons. But modernization of the RVNAF proceeded slowly because the U.S. forces took over the task of opposing the major NVA formations and MACV did not initially strongly advocate new weapons and equipment for the RVNAF. The exception was the growth and modernization of the Vietnamese Air Force (VNAF). F-5 fighters were supplied to the VNAF in June 1967, followed by A-37's in August. AC-47 "Spooky" gunships were issued to the VNAF in November 1969. These planes were to provide support for ground operations in the South rather than to prepare the air battle with the North Vietnamese Air Force, which had had Mig-15s and Mig-17s since February 1965, and Mig-21s later on.

The upgrading of the Navy during this period was insignificant; all patrol and surveillance missions at sea and on rivers were being performed by the U.S. Navy. Mine clearing became an Amrican responsibility in March 1966 and American mobile riverine units began operations in the Mekong Delta in January 1967.

In this period (1965-67) the Army received no significant new weapons or materiel. The replacement of M-24 tanks by M-41 tanks progressed at a snail's pace. Infantry units were still equipped with M-1 rifles, and M-1 and M-2 carbines. Only the Airborne and Marine Divisions were equipped with M-16 rifles; the only infantry unit with these weapons was the 2d Regiment on the DMZ.

Vietnamization gave new impetus to the modernization of the RVNAF. Both Vietnamese and American leaders considered it essential that RVNAF gradually replace U.S. forces as well as match the enemy's modernization effort in the South. Small arms such as M-16 rifles, M-60 machine guns, M-79 grenade launchers, M-72 LAW rockets were issued to infantry units. After the operations in Laos of February 1971, the Army was equipped with M-48 tanks and 175-mm guns.

The 1972 Communist offensive led to further advances with *Enhance*, which expedited the modernization process providing anti-tank TOW rockets, additional M-48 tanks to activate two armored battalions, each with 54 tanks, and more 175-mm guns to activate three additional heavy artillery battalions. The Air Force received more transports such as C-119's, C-123's and C-7's. The Navy was supplied additional boats and ships.

In November 1972, when the Paris peace talks were showing signs of progress toward a cease-fire agreement, *Enhance Plus* was the last-ditch effort to modernize the RVNAF before restrictions were imposed by the Paris treaty. Materiel flowed in at an accelerated rate by both sea and air. Under this program the Marines got 31 additional NVT-5 amphibious vehicles; the Air Force was increased by three A-37 squadrons, two F-5A squadrons, one UH-1 helicopter squadron, one AC-119K squadron, and two C-130 squadrons (replacing C-123's). In the period from 23 October to 12 December 1972, 5,000 short tons of equipment and supplies were moved by air and 100,000 by sea under this program.

Throughout the period covering from the First Republic to the Paris agreement signed on 27 January 1973, the modernization process had equipped the RVNAF with powerful and modern weaponry, but in 1971, when presented with GVN requests for first-rate weapons systems such as F-101 and F-4 fighters, MACV turned them down. GVN requests for modernization were approved only if they were considered by MACV to be essential and did not involve excessively sophisticated weapons; requests that were made in anticipation of future needs were rejected. These rejections, far from stirring up strong resentment on the part of GVN authorities, reinforced everybody's confidence in the long-term presence and support of the United States.

The possibility that the U.S. and allied forces would someday withdraw and that the U.S. support would greatly diminish should have been matters of concern to those who were responsible for formulating national strategies. Yet Vietnamese leaders held to the notion that the announced U.S. withdrawal would be only a partial one. Consequently, even after the Midway Conference, during which the new strategy was advanced for a gradual American withdrawal, President Thieu did not initiate any national plan to face this eventuality. No decisions or instructions emanated from the Independence Palace after this conference.

Vietnamization as a term and as a concept was far more important in American politics than it was to the average Vietnamese. In fact, if it hadn't received a great deal of publicity, promoted by the Americans, few Vietnamese would have even heard of it. So far as the Joint General Staff was concerned, which was never briefed on the concept or given guidance by the President, the important event was the expansion and modernization of the RVNAF to meet the growing threat from the North. If the Americans wanted to call that *Vietnamization* it was alright and any senior Vietnamese official was happy to participate in any well-publicized top-level conference with the Americans to discuss this or any other concept. He would gladly put his name to American-drafted proclamations of great purpose because this would serve to enhance his prestige in the eyes of the people and diminish the power of his political opposition.

The trouble with these Vietnamese attitudes was that they missed the vital point: a new strategy had been announced by the Americans. *Vietnamization* was more than modernization and expansion of the RVNAF; it was essentially a strategy that would require the Vietnamese to survive with greatly reduced American participation. Had President Thieu and the Joint General Staff fully realized this fact, perhaps they would have begun then to build a strategy to cope with it. Instead, the RVNAF made no adjustments in doctrine, organization or training to compensate for the departure of American troops and firepower.

As a matter of fact, the North Vietnamese reacted much more positively to *Vietnamization* than did the Southerners. They feared that it would succeed to the extend that a Northern military victory would become increasingly more difficult. Largely for this reason, they launched the 1972 offensive to preempt such success.

The 1972 offensive was followed by the Paris agreement which required the absolute withdrawal of American forces, leaving the Republic of Vietnam struggling to find a strategy for survival under new and forbidding circumstances.

The Problem of Survival

The Communist general offensive of the summer of 1973 closed with a cease-fire treaty, a peace agreement. No responsible leader in the South believed, however, that this peace was permanent; war would sooner or later break out again. This peace treaty brought about the withdrawal of all U.S. and allied forces from Vietnam, but did not even discuss the North Vietnamese troops in the South. From then on the balance of military power gradually tipped in favor of North Vietnam.[2] The South Vietnamese leadership knew this but was comforted by the expectation that strong support from the United States—in terms of military and economic aid and, if necessary, the application of American airpower—would be forthcoming to redress the imbalance if North Vietnam resumed hostilities.

On President Thieu's order, a delegation from the JGS headed by Lieutenant General Le Nguyen Khang, Chief of Operations, visited each Military Region to relay to each corps commander instructions to draw up contingency military plans in case of renewed hostilities. These plans were drafted on the assumption that American air support and intervention would be available, especially by B-52 bombers, two to three weeks after the war resumed.

---

[2] For more detail concerning the enemy's strategy during the post-cease-fire period see Chapter III of the Final Collapse by General Cao Van Vien.

National objectives remained unchanged. The RVNAF was charged to regain control of territory that the Communists had captured soon after the cease-fire, to defend occupied territories, and to protect the people. In the confrontations with the NVA that arose the RVNAF methods of fighting until February 1974 were unchanged; great reliance was placed on fire superiority and mobility. Losses in materiel and expenditures of ammunition had not yet become a matter of concern because of the promise of one-for-one replacement by the U.S. as authorized by the Paris agreement. The JGS expected American aid to diminish over time, but clung to the belief -- based on American assurances -- that significant aid cuts would not occur until a genuine peace had been achieved.

At the beginning of 1973, President Thieu instructed the Defense Ministry and the JGS to study a troop reduction plan according to which each military region would retain only one division on active duty; the general reserve under JGS control would be two divisions. All other divisions would be reduced to cadre strength. Reserve officers, noncommissioned officers and enlisted men would be gradually discharged and revert to inactive reserve status. They would be subject to annual training periods and called to active duty only when hostilities should resume. This study was completed but orders implementing it were never issued because the premise of peace never materialized.

The U.S. decision to reduce military aid to Vietnam during the 1974 fiscal year was made known to the Defense Attache Office, Saigon (DAO) by the end of September 1973 and was relayed by DAO to JGS in January 1974. By February the JGS had directed combat units to economize on ammunition expenditures but no strict restrictions were imposed. The reluctance to apply drastic measures was in part due to the abiding faith in the ability of the U.S. Administration to sway Congress, and in part to the desire to avert a shock wave from engulfing the armed forces and spreading to the general population.

Meanwhile, first-rate materiel of the Vietnamese Navy and Air Force was not being replaced as anticipated. For a loss of 281 airplanes which the Air Force had suffered since the cease-fire until the end of 1974 it received only eight O-1's in replacement. The Navy lost a total of 58 vessels and received none. Only 49 percent of authorized motor vehicles in the RVNAF were still serviceable for lack of spare parts.

In order to live with the cut in military assistance and the plan to develop the nation's economy, the government projected a troop reduction of 100,000. This reduction was to begin in July 1974, affecting first all non-combat units, which could fill only to 85% of their authorized strength. No soldiers were ever discharged under the plan because authorized strengths were below the ceiling already. Since the military situation kept worsening day by day, the 100,000 troop slash was abandoned in September 1974.

Now that a reduction in personnel could not be carried out, consumption and use of equipment had to be restricted. The Air Force received orders to bring the number of active squadrons from 66 down to 56 and 224 airplanes of all kinds were inactivated. Flying time was reduced; fuel and spare parts supplies were at 65% of 1973 levels. The Navy took a cut from 44 to 24 boat units. The artillery could no longer fire harassment and interdiction fire and daily allowances for 105-mm artillery came to eight rounds per tube as compared to 30 rounds in 1972; for 175-mm guns the allowance was one round per piece per day. Mortars in outposts could fire no more than three rounds. Soldiers who used to be issued six grenades on each operation now received two. Stories of RF and PF units in IV Corps buying grenades out of their pocket money were, though incredible, nevertheless true.

Such conditions prompted President Thieu to say that the RVNAF had to learn to fight a "poor man's war"; what this poor man's war should entail, however, was never made clear. Its meaning could be reduction in fuel and ammunition consumption, fewer large-scale operations, more small-scale actions in their place, and more commando-type actions. But President Thieu never issed such guidance. Old combat tactics were no longer suitable to the new situation. What would new tactics be like? The task of finding a new way of fighting was assigned to a field manual drafting committee in the Agency for Military Training composed of representatives of JGS divisions and of the combat arms and services. This project achieved little. The difficulty encountered by the committee was to devise a new war doctrine with a purely Vietnamese character, as contrasted with the prevailing doctrine which was patterned after U.S. doctrine. But the committee members had experience only as fighters of a rich man's war. And even if new tactics could be articulated, their adoption would run into difficulties. For better or for worse, poor man's tactics would be regarded as evidence of a decline in military strength. This feeling of decline would have a profound effect on troop morale in combat. Second, relinquishing the old ways of fighting would prove far from easy; few soldiers would like the idea of medical evacuation by man-packed litter or truck, having gotten used to evacuation by helicopter. The same reaction would apply with respect to fire support provided by organic mortars versus that provided by air. Besides, it would require time for the troops to acquire the needed endurance and training. For example, while formerly reconnaissance units would be brought to or removed from objective areas by helicopter, were supplied with adequate and nutritious canned rations, now they would have to go overland and be weighted down with heavier unprocessed foods and heavier equipment. Everything had to be revised from scratch; from the training conducted in school to the practice in the field.

Other significant problems were the inevitable comparison with the enemy; not a comparison in terms of means, for the RVNAF still had air power at their disposal while the Communists did not, but a comparison of trends. While Communist forces were becoming better equipped and more modernized day by day, RVNAF was heading on a downward slide.

Another comparison occurred with respect to the society as a whole in its multifarious aspects. The stark contrast between the constrained and spare life of the military and the luxurious and wasteful way of life of city dwellers could not easily be reconciled.

In addition to all these difficulties, there was the question of whether newly conceived tactics would be effective, and whether the the enemy would allow RVNAF enough time for the transformation to take place.

These tough problems forced President Thieu into rethinking his strategic position and contemplating territorial defense more commensurate with capabilities. This he once briefly revealed in a meeting of the National Security Council called to review the military situation at the beginning of 1974. In that meeting President Thieu instructed the military region commanders to have ready a plan to abandon part of their territory should it become indefensible, and to determine which part of the territory to relinquish should the need arise. Despite their utmost importance, these instructions were never officially renewed or confirmed and no military region commander obeyed them.

CHAPTER IV

United States' Influence on Republic of Vietnam's Strategy

Many observers of the Vietnam war have assumed that because South Vietnam was totally dependent on the United States for the necessary means to defend itself, and because United States forces from 1965 to 1968 assumed direct operational responsibilities, that the military strategy of the Republic of Vietnam must have closely paralleled that of the United States. It is true that under these circumstances U.S. influence could not help but be pervasive. In fact, a survey of the situation in the South from 1954 to 1975 reveals that American influence on the South's strategy varied in direct ratio to the nature and extent of American involvement and assistance in Vietnam.

American Influence in the Pre-Intervention Period

As the leaders of the First Republic assumed the reins of government and the responsibilities for defense, one fact was paramount in their minds: the various factions and sects that each controlled a segment of the nation's military force had to be subdued and the direction of the military effort had to be centralized in the office of the president.

Secondly the Vietnamese leadership realized that the peace just concluded at Geneva could be temporary; that a future war was possible and that the conflict would be either an invasion from the North, or an insurgency in the South, or a combination of both. If the country were to be adequately prepared, something had to be done immediately to fill the vacuum left by the departure of the French forces which numbered 235,000 men. The government believed that a national army of 216,000 —

its strength in 1954—would be required for the defense tasks facing the First Republic.

It was at this point that the first American influence was exerted on the shaping of South Vietnam's military strategy. This influence is recorded in detail in the *Understanding on Development and Training of Autonomous Vietnam Armed Forces*, executed between General J. Lawton Collins and the Government of Vietnam in December 1954.[1] The American view expressed in this document was that South Vietnam needed only the forces required to defeat insurgency; the army would be required to delay an invasion from the North only until SEATO could come to its assistance. For this mission, the Americans would fund a defense establishment of up to 100,000 men.

The Americans also suggested the structure of the Republic's armed forces in some detail. There would be three territorial divisions with a total of 13 security regiments, each with three security battalions. These divisions were the core of the anti-guerrilla force. They would also authorize three field divisions, the force that would delay the North Vietnamese until SEATO would intervene. The general reserve would be one airborne regimental combat team.

In April 1955, the MAAG proposed a timetable for demobilizing the national army in order to get it down to the 100,000-man limit imposed by the funding limitations. Under this plan, the National Army would be reduced to 150,000 by 1 May 1955; to 125,000 by August 1955; and down to 100,000 by 1 November 1955. The plan to reduce troop strength had to be carried out hastily in order to meet the first deadline of 1 May 1955. At this time ARVN was in the process of reorganization and needed large headquarters elements and support units to execute the reorganization. Therefore, the demobilization

---

[1] File 204-58 (281-45) Org. Planning Files. Functions, Missions and Command Relationships (1963).

could not be allowed to cut into these specialized troops; that left only combat troops to be discharged and the first demobilization phase affected these elements, but it was the only option available at that time. During the period 1955 to 1958, over 6,000 well-trained and battle-experienced noncommissioned officers who had large families were hastily and obligatorily discharged. There was no plan under consideration to assist them to readjust to civilian life, not even a retirement pension because at the time no such military statute was on the books.

The effects of these discharges were not thought out or evaluated at the time but showed up clearly in the way counter-insurgency operations were conducted in later years; combat efficiency noticeably decreased compared with previous years. And one of the reasons was that the newly trained officers and noncommissioned officers lacked the experience of the old leaders who had been discharged. Furthermore, the demobilization of combat troops adversely affected the morale of those who were allowed to remain in service because they considered the forced discharges as unconscionable acts on the part of an ungrateful government.

Another American concept promoted by the MAAG during this period was that only a small regular army was required, one that could be rapidly expanded in time of war through a draft of trained reservists. The Vietnamese had no experience with this system and preferred a large standing army of volunteers. The government of Vietnam held that it needed a largely voluntary standing army with few draftees, and conceived of national defense as requiring capabilities to secure areas as well as engaging in mobile defense. Area security, in the government's view, required the activation of regional regiments recruited in local communities and operating in local areas; local recruits would be familiar with the terrain, loyal to their native region, and would give the fullest measure of devotion to their duties. The American view was that the army needed a great deal of mobility, a large number of specialists, and draftees. The MAAG opposed the idea of regional units because regional units would not be strategically mobile. A compromise was finally reached whereby each province would have at least one territorial battalion.

The United States also approved three territorial divisions but while the discussions were going on, Vietnam put together the fourth division, presenting the United States with a *fait accompli*.

The effect of the first wave of discharges and the commotion it created in the army and among the people of the South was alleviated when in June 1955 the MAAG approved a 150,000-man army composed of ten infantry divisions, six field and four light. The field divisions were to confront invasions from the North in conventional warfare. The light divisions were to have the capability of conducting counter-insurgency in mobile warfare while fulfilling a supporting role toward field divisions.

In 1958, all light divisions were disbanded because in the judgment of General Samuel Williams, Chief of the MAAG, they would be no match for regular NVA divisions. Out of the ten divisions, seven identical infantry divisions were formed.

General Williams may have been correct with regard to the inability of the light divisions to handle conventional combat against North Vietnamese regular divisions, but his insistence on forming heavy infantry divisions to deal with them made it apparent that the Americans estimated that SEATO would not be capable of intervening in time if there was an invasion from the North. If not, why should the South organize to repel an invasion rather than simply delay until SEATO forces could be deployed? In any case, while the new infantry divisions might eventually be capable of the mission they were being designed for, there were no light, mobile units to move rapidly into remote, difficult terrain against the guerrillas. And by 1959 the guerrilla threat was growing serious and was, in fact, the only active threat to the nation's security.

President Diem recognized this problem and his administration did something about it. In early 1960, the government ordered each infantry battalion in ARVN to organize one additional company to use in the war against the insurgents. The companies consisted of battle-experienced, tough troopers, who were lightly equipped and dressed, much the same as their VC adversaries. They wore the black pajamas and *Binh Tri Thien* sandals and could move quickly and quietly into battle against the VC.[2] These companies, formed without MAAG approval, were the origin of the Vietnamese Rangers whose support was picked up by the MAAG in 1961 when the training mission was assigned to the U.S. 5th Special Forces.

Besides the differences in views on regular forces, the MAAG and the government of the First Republic differed on how the Civil Guard and Self-Defense Corps should be organized and controlled. The U.S. concept was manifested in the training program conducted by the Michigan State University Group (MSUG) in Vietnam; the Civil Guard was to be a kind of rural police, equipped with nothing heavier than sub-machine guns, and organized into small units. The Vietnamese wanted this organization to be a paramilitary force with the capability to assist regular forces and to be organized into large units strong enough to handle actions against local insurgent units.

The desire to strengthen the Civil Guard (and U.S. reluctance to do so) prompted President Diem to negotiate for assistance with Malaysian Prime Minister Tunku Abdul Rahman. The result was a 1960 Malaysian gift to Vietnam of about 600 armored cars of the Ford Lynx and Scout car types for highway security, and 60 Wickham Trolley cars for railroad security. All went to equip the Civil Guard. Additionally, 200,000 shotguns were supplied to the Self-Defense Corps. President Diem was also able to obtain from the Colombo Plan a number of Landrover Jeeps and signal equipment for the Civil Guard.

The Americans eventually came around to the Vietnamese view with regard to the missions and organization of the Civil Guard and the Self-Defense Corps, but the matter of authority over these forces was still an issue in 1960 when the training and equipping of the Civil Guard was transferred by the Americans from the Economic Aid Mission (USOM) to the MAAG. According to the Americans, the Civil Guard and Self-Defense Corps should be transferred from the Ministry of Interior to the Ministry of

---

[2] *Binh Tri Thien* sandals were the traditional footwear of the VC. Made of sections of rubber tires with inner-tube thongs, their name came from three provinces where the VC were originally strong: Quang *Binh*, Quang *Tri*, and Thua *Thien*.

Three Wickham Trolleys on the Saigon-Bien Hoa Railway, 1965

Defense so that they would respond better to military command. President
Diem did not subscribe to this theory. His pragmatic position was that
he could better control the internal affairs of the country by placing the
Civil Guard and Self-Defense Forces under his Minister of Interior. He
foresaw a potentially unstable condition if he centered too much power and
authority in his generals. Furthermore, Counselor Ngo Dinh Nhu had made
it clear on many occasions — during his periodic meetings with the Joint
General Staff — that he considered the country's military leadership to
be weak, lacking in leadership, and unschooled in strategy and tactics.
In short, the military was not capable of assuming responsibility for the
para-military forces. Nevertheless, responding to pressure from the MAAG,
President Diem signed an order in 1961 placing the Civil Guard and Self-
Defense Corps under the Ministry of Defense. In fact, however, nothing
had changed. The province chiefs, who controlled the local forces as sector
commanders and through their sub-sector commanders, still responded to
the Minister of Interior.

During the years of the First Republic, while the influence of
American ideas and American systems was strong in Vietnam, the Vietnamese
also looked elsewhere for inspiration and assistance; witness President
Diem's contacts with the Colombo Plan and Tunku Abdul Rahman. Another
source of influence came out of Malaysia in the person of Sir Robert
Thompson. Sir Robert had had considerable experience in the successful
British anti-guerrilla campaign in Malaysia and, at the request of
President Diem, he brought a small team of advisers to Vietnam. He
became the government's police, security, and political warfare adviser.

Another example of the Diem Administration's attempt to avoid becoming excessively dependent on American advice and assistance was his
effort to establish an ammunition factory at Cat Lai in Gia Dinh Province.
In 1958 a Vietnamese ordnance delegation visited Japan to investigate
the feasibility of buying the equipment for such a plant.

Despite such attempts to preserve its independence, however, the
imitation of American ways became a fad with many ranking Vietnamese
officers. A case in point was the adoption of American-style uniforms.

In 1956, Lieutenant General Le Van Ty, Chief of the Joint General Staff addressed the staff officers as follows:

> "In my opinion, for combat uniforms we should retain the bush hat because it is far better suited to the tropical and rainy climate of our country than the U.S. visor cap. Fatigues too would be better to have two thigh pockets to provide for more carrying capacity for combat troops. However, since you Chiefs of Staff of the Armed Forces want to adopt American models, I too will be with you on the bandwagon."

United States Army training methods and concepts came in with the U.S. Army advisers in 1955 and were adopted by the ARVN. Command and leadership courses were held to retrain officers and noncommissioned officers in everything from the U.S. Army manual-of-arms for the rifle to combat tactics and marksmanship with American weapons. These matters were not too difficult for Vietnamese soldiers to accept, but the rigid, harsh, American-style discipline of the training camp went down hard. It was just not the Vietnamese way to require such emphasis on saluting and spit-and-polish, and to punish officers and soldiers with push-ups for minor infractions of discipline or poor performance.

Two other concepts of training brought by the Americans to Vietnam also caused some difficulties. One was the American insistence that 20-mile marches for soldiers carrying battle-gear weighing 30 pounds or more was good training. The painful fact was that the average Vietnamese soldier wasn't built for that kind of exertion in the tropics. The other was the idea that unit training cycles should conclude with regimental and division level maneuvers in order to fully exercise the commanders and staffs at these echelons. The trouble was that the war was being fought at that time against small guerrilla bands and these maneuvers were not only irrelevant but they diverted the troops from active combat responsibilities.

In summary, the American advisers during the First Republic greatly influenced the strategies and methods adopted by the Vietnamese armed forces, but were always ready to compromise and defer to the Vietnamese viewpoint when it became necessary. Perhaps this was a reflection of President Kennedy's stated philosophy to the effect that the United

States would provide the means, but the Vietnamese should fight their war in their own way.

Americanization

With time American influence became deeper, especially after the replacement of the First Republic by a succession of governments between 1964 and 1966. The Vietnamese leadership had practically nothing new to propose while the strategy, except for modifications of the First Republic's Strategic Hamlet program, became Americanized.

In the years from 1965 to 1969, when U.S. forces assumed an active fighting role in Vietnam, military strategy originated at MACV. The RVNAF accepted the responsibility for pacification of populated areas while American forces carried out search-and-destroy missions in Communist base areas and along their lines of communication. Other American units worked along the border to prevent infiltration. This strategy of dividing the tasks between the U.S. forces and the RVNAF resulted in heavy Communist losses but the VCI remained very active and effective.

The destruction of the VCI had been high on the Diem government's priorities but largely escaped American attention during that period. The reactivation of the effort in the *Phoenix* program by the Americans was another instance of Americanization, at least as seen by Vietnamese.

When American military forces entered the Vietnamese battlefields in 1965, the South Vietnamese were dazzled by the efficient organization, the abundant resources, the prompt execution of orders, and the modern, scientific techniques displayed by U.S. forces. It quickly became the ambition of most RVNAF leaders to emulate U.S. forces in organization, equipment and operations. Quite naturally, coordination at all levels between Vietnamese and American staffs and units demanded identity of organization and modes of operation. Field units had to follow U.S. procedures for requesting fire support and RVNAF logistical installations had to follow uniform management procedures. Americanization was dictated by practical realities; it was an irresistible current. Even small units, such as PF platoons or RF companies in Military Region 1, felt the impact of Americanization through their participation in the U.S. Marines' CAT program.

Another very important factor leading to Americanization was the activity of U.S. advisers in Vietnamese units. U.S. coaching pervaded and influenced Vietnamese unit leaders and gradually spread to the soldiers themselves.

Besides the effect of Americanization on the appearance of the RVNAF and on its equipment and methods of fighting, another effect was much more subtle but of far greater strategic importance: the Americans had designed a purely defensive strategy for Vietnam. It was a strategy that was based on attrition of the enemy through a prolonged defense and made no allowance for decisive offensive action.

General Westmoreland wrote about American strategy in Vietnam under the Johnson Administration as follows:

> "Hold the enemy, defeat him in the South, help build a nation, bomb war-related targets in the North on a gradually escalating basis until the enemy gets the message that he cannot win, and then will negotiate or tacitly accept a divided Vietnam."[3]

U.S. Ambassador Goldberg affirmed this to a session of the United Nations General Assembly in 1966:

> "We do not seek to overthrow the government of North Vietnam. We do not demand of North Vietnam an unconditional surrender, or anything related to it."

This American strategy of gradual escalation was commented on in 1967 by North Vietnamese General Van Tien Dung:

> "He (the enemy) escalated step by step out of worry. He fights while applying pressure on us. His escalation depends on the development of the war situation in the South and on his diplomatic plots. Therefore, now they escalate, now they deescalate, then escalate again to a notch higher."[4]

---

[3] William C. Westmoreland, <u>Vietnam in Perspective</u>, (a speech delivered by General Westmoreland on several occasions during 1976 and 1977).

[4] "Great Victory, Great Mission" in People's Daily, (North Vietnam undated).

Vo Nguyen Giap observed that the reason the U.S. imposed restrictions on targets in the North was to prevent the Vietnam war from adversely affecting political, economic, social, and diplomatic objectives of the United States. In other words, the American strategy, according to Giap, was designed to accomplish American objectives. If those objectives happened to coincide with the best interests of South Vietnam, the U.S.-Vietnam alliance was a fortunate one. If not, it was not at all clear that the American strategy was the best for South Vietnam. Nevertheless given that U.S. support and intervention was at that time critical to the survival of South Vietnam, the leaders of the South had no rational alternative but to accept American leadership in strategy. But this did not mean that there were no voices in dissent offering other strategic ideas. In 1965, when U.S. forces started pouring into the South, the Minister of Defense, General Cao Van Vien, wrote a paper entitled "The Strategy of Isolation" in which he likened the task of stopping infiltration to that of turning off the faucet of a water tank. General Vien advocated turning off the faucet through the isolation of North Vietnam. He would fortify a zone along the 17th parallel from Dong Ha to Savannakhet and follow this with a landing operation at Vinh or Ha Tinh, just north of the 18th parallel, cutting off the North's front from its rear. In 1972 General Vien published the original paper with the following added conclusions: "In her alliance with the United States, Vietnam was hamstrung in her action, causing her strategy to be confined to the defensive."[5]

No such strategy as proposed by General Vien could have been adopted without United States approval. In the first place, the RVNAF were not equipped or trained to undertake a major amphibious operation; U.S. forces would have to participate. Secondly, if the South Vietnamese were to attempt such a thing on their own in defiance of American policy, they would shortly find all support from the United States abruptly terminated. That was understood.

---

[5]"The Strategy of Isolation," in Military Review, U.S. Army Command and General Staff College, April 1972, p. 23.

The American defensive-gradual escalation strategy was not only clearly stated by American leaders, it was demonstrated in concrete terms to the South Vietnamese through the military assistance program. In 1974, for example, the most modern planes available to the Vietnamese Air Force were F-5As, and A-37s. Although the RVNAF had, in their modernization plans for the years 1969-1972, requested F-104 and F-105 jet fighters, these requests were refused with the explanation that the U.S. Air Force would always be present to provide this sort of capability for South Vietnam.

The RVNAF was equipped with modern weapons only after comparable ones had been employed by the enemy. M-16 rifles were supplied to all RVNAF units only after the 1968 *Tet* Offensive when the enemy employed Communist AK-47s in large numbers. Only after the 1971 operation in Laos (*Lam Son 719*) were M-48 tanks supplied to meet the enemy's T-54s, and 175-mm self-propelled guns were furnished to counterbalance the Communist 130-mm guns. Following the 1972 summer offensive, TOW anti-tank missiles were supplied after the Communists had employed AT-3 anti-tank missiles. These modern American weapons were furnished only after the Communists had used theirs on a large scale and had gained military and psychological advantages in doing so.

The Americans, as we have seen, eventually dictated the grand strategy of the conflict. With their monopoly over weaponry and equipment, they also shaped how that strategy would be executed, what tactics and techniques would be employed. It was only a small step to providing the actual impetus and direction to major RVNAF and joint military operations. The Cambodian foray in 1970 and the Laos operation to Tchepone in 1971 came into being only because MACV originated them, promoted them and supported them.

When the Laos operation ran into difficulty because the North Vietnamese committed their general reserve divisions, MACV proposed throwing an additional Vietnamese infantry division into the fray. The commander of the 2d ARVN Division was even told by his American adviser to prepare for deployment. President Thieu, however, after meeting with his military staff, decided that the commitment of one more division not only would

Soviet Assault Rifles (AK-47) captured during the 1970 Cambodian Incursion on public display

not improve the situation but would result in heavier losses. Thereupon, he issued orders that this division would not deploy to Laos.

This and other incidents illustrated the fact that despite the strong American influence during the period of American participation in the war, the allies had a few areas of disagreement. One of the issues of most serious conflict involved the fundamental organization of the armed forces. Whereas MACV always advocated expanding Regional Forces at the expense of the regular forces, the government held to the opposite view and wanted the regular army enlarged and modernized. The American argument was that the cost of a RF unit was considerably less than that of a comparable regular unit. The government conceded that but thought that the added effectiveness of the regular unit was worth it.

American Influence After Withdrawal

After the Paris agreement was signed on 28 January 1973, the actual presence of U.S. forces ceased but U.S. influence persisted almost intact with its impact on the strategy and its execution. In national defense, from organization to operations, from training to combat methods and the utilization of resources and ammunition, nothing much changed until July 1974. Then, confronted by the stark and obvious realities of the decrease in U.S. military assistance, the South sought to find a new strategy to face the deteriorating military situation and the austere budgetary limits.

This matter of dealing with the priorities of a defense budget was a new experience for the RVNAF staff. During the years before the withdrawal of MACV, the RVNAF involvement with the defense budget ended with the presentation of its military requirements. MACV took it from there and determined the priorities and unilaterally managed the execution of the budget. This was the system despite repeated requests made by the RVNAF J-4 to the MACV J-4 that the RVNAF should participate in the entire budgetary process in the interests of more accurate assessments of requirements and greater efficiency and economy. Finally, as the urgency for belt-tightening became apparent, the JGS was invited by MACV's successor, the Defense Attache Office, to get involved. What the Chief of Logistics of the RVNAF was unable to determine at the time was whether this change was due to a shift in American policy or simply because Major General John Murray, the Defense Attache, took it upon himself to do so.

In any event, faced with severe cuts in ammunition stocks, fuel and spare parts, the RVNAF had to take a fresh look at how it would continue to fight the war. It could no longer afford the old techniques that relied so heavily on massed firepower and helicopter-mobility.

But time was running short. Furthermore, large battles were being joined and a change of course at this time would be as difficult as "switching horses in midstream." In fact, the attempt to adopt new tactics and techniques had only begun when the Communist attacked Ban Me Thuot.

The loss of Ban Me Thuot impelled a change in strategy. From the policy and slogan of "Hold All," President Thieu switched to that of "Hold the southern half," leaving the northern half of the country undefended. This unexpected change in strategy was never publicly explained by President Thieu and was thought of by the great majority of the people, by the armed forces, and even by high-ranking military officers as the implementation of a secret agreement worked out at the Paris peace talks between the U.S. and North Vietnam, which the government of the South, under tremendous U.S. pressure, had to carry out. Others speculated that it was President Thieu's ploy to force the United States into continuing the commitment it had contracted toward Vietnam. If so, the move failed and the result of this astounding miscalculation was the downfall of the republican form of government and freedom in South Vietnam.

CHAPTER V

The Tactics of the Republic of Vietnam Armed Forces

The First Steps

Born in 1950, the National Army of Vietnam, the parent of the Republic of Vietnam Armed Forces, had only a few infantry battalions and airborne battalions in its regular force in all of Vietnam. In 1950 and 1951 all battalion commanders and some company commanders were French officers. In 1952 Vietnamese battalion commanders began to assume command and a few battalions had exclusively Vietnamese officers, such as the 16th and 18th Battalions in Bui Chu-Phat Diem, and the 4th and 10th Battalions in Hung Yen.

Of course the tactics of the National Army were based on French doctrine. Vietnamese officers attended the Tong and Nam Dinh military schools in North Vietnam and Thu Duc, Nuoc Ngot, and Dalat in the South. French instructors staffed the schools and used the field manuals of the French Army. Once assigned to the field, their association with French officers and cooperation with French units naturally influenced Vietnamese officers to adopt the French tactics and techniques for conducting conventional warfare.

In this period some National Army units were employed to man outposts in rural localities. Other units were used in mobile operations in coordination with French units. The latter was the case with the airborne and infantry battalions in mobile groups (*Groupes Mobiles*).

In outpost-manning missions, Vietnamese battalions were usually employed by company groups or companies. Assisted by Civil Guard companies or supplementary forces, outpost units were given the routine, daily mission of clearing roads connecting one outpost to another and maintaining highway security. The only techniques they learned were those used in road-clearing and security. Each post was assigned an area of responsibility half-way to the adjacent outpost. Every morning troops would be sent out to clear the roads of mines that had been laid in the roadway during the night and to detect enemy ambushes. When units of the two adjacent posts met and nothing else happened, the road was considered open. The troops remained along the road to maintain security until evening when they pulled back to their camps and the road was once again closed.

Day in-day out, the same units started on their road-clearing missions on the same road at the same time through the same terrain; the techniques remained constant. Rifle squads would deploy on both sides of the road. Following them, other rifle squads and mine-detection teams would walk on the road to clear every meter of road of mines and obstacles. About 200 meters to the rear the machine gun squad and the platoon or company command element followed with signal personnel to maintain contact with the outpost. They were able to call for mortar or artillery support when needed.

It may be thought that since road-clearing missions had become so routine that units fell into ambushes out of negligence and complacency. It wasn't really that way. Even though each unit had done the same thing hundreds of times, they approached each mission with great seriousness and caution. Although the distances covered were short and the terrain was familiar, danger and the unexpected lurked everywhere most of the time. Visibility was impaired on both sides of the road by high grass, jungle or the immense rice paddies. The enemy used mines and booby traps in profusion and spikes and nails that pierced feet were another constant hazard. On jungle trails the troops would walk in the footprints of the preceding men but in the lowlands this technique could not be used because line formations were needed to cover wide areas.

No matter how cautious road clearing units were, they could not avoid losses in ambushes because the enemy was in control of the factors that guaranteed success; surprise, cover and concealment and good intelligence. He rarely had to worry about the reaction of the units being ambushed because supporting firepower or reinforcements were usually not immediately available. Reaction by artillery, armor or reinforcements

would be available only if road-clearing missions were conducted at
least at the province level.

Missions at the province/sector level were conducted ordinarily only
to open the road for resupply of isolated outposts beyond the range of
small units. These operations were usually conducted by company groups
or battalions. Troops employed would be the sector's regular mobile
battalion, commando companies, the Civil Guard and auxiliary forces
stationed in the province. Even though these road-clearing missions
had greater strength and more support, they also could not avoid ambushes.
Here again the enemy had a clear advantage, especially in intelligence.
He could estimate quite accurately when the sector would have to undertake such a mission because he knew the status of supply in the outposts
being resupplied.

Besides their road-clearing and resupply missions to remote and
isolated outposts, the sector's mobile battalion was used in relief
missions to outposts under attack and to attack enemy units when their
locations were discovered by intelligence sources.

Clearing the enemy from villages in North or Central Vietnam differed
in many ways from such operations in villages in the South. Villages in
North and Central Vietnam were usually clusters of hundreds of houses
surrounded by large bamboo groves. The village's edges were dotted with
scattered graves. There were usually only one or two main roads into a
typical village. Inside the village, the roads (often only paths) twisted
and curved from one house to the next or from one cluster of houses to
another. The opportunities for concealment and ambush were almost endless.
Furthermore, maps were scarce and showed villages only in rough form.
To make matters worse, many of these villages had no government or were
under hostile control.

Clearing operations in villages such as these had to be improvised
to suit the situation. Half the work would be considered done if the
operating troops reached the village edge, a very important achievement.
At least a force the size of a battalion was usually required. Company
size missions could achieve their objectives only if enemy contact was
not made or made only with scattered guerrilla elements. Searching the

village proved to be most difficult. In 1953, during *Operation Brochet* in Hung Yen, the search unit was a crack airborne battalion. For three days in the village there was no contact, but on the third night the enemy swarmed out of his underground hideouts and inflicted heavy casualties on the battalion.

In 1953, newly created Vietnamese rifle battalions were taken to Bui Chu (in North Vietnam) for testing their operational capability in clearing and pacification actions using the "harrowing technique." The battalions combed a large area in the same way a giant harrow would take a piece of land. The technique failed, however, because the units were green, their equipment was inferior, their fighting spirit nonexistent, and the ability of adjacent units to rescue one another minimal.

Vietnamese units that were accustomed to and fairly effective in outpost duty proved to be weak when operating outside their bases. Outposts were usually square fortifications with a main bunker on each corner. The walls and barricades were made of wood, bamboo and earth, while the bunkers were usually concrete. One consideration in the location of these fortifications was mutual fire support. An outpost might have two or three barbed wire fences, depending on its importance. Firepower was provided by 81-mm mortars, 60-mm mortars, grenade launchers and automatic rifles. The more important posts also had 12.7-mm machine guns. Besides signal equipment, there were pyrotechnics to signal neighboring posts when under attack.

There were many instances where, after half of the outposts had collapsed, the remaining fortified positions fought on for three days until reinforcements or relief by infantry troops and artillery or airpower forced the enemy to withdraw. It was noteworthy that the defense of outposts was not taught in military schools and a number of troops that manned their defense, who came from auxiliary forces and the Civil Guard, had practically no training at all. Nevertheless, there were many instances of creative ideas generated by individual soldiers in these outposts. One post commander, when his outpost came under pressure, had replicas of 120-mm mortars made from paper and spread the word among the populace that the post had newly acquired firepower. Another, when he lost contact with higher headquarters, simulated receiving orders and communications in order to maintain troop morale and deter enemy attacks. The defense of outposts was based more on the experience troops gained on the job than on the field manuals.

Road security, clearing operations and outpost defense employed routine techniques the Vietnamese units used from the beginning of the war until the end. It was not until the RVNAF were equipped with armored personnel carriers and helicopters that new techniques appeared.

A New Direction

In April 1955 the MAAG assumed the training of the RVNAF infantry. Courses were offered at Fort Benning and Fort Leavenworth for Vietnamese officers. The majority of ranking generals of the RVNAF, including President Nguyen Van Thieu and General Cao Van Vien, were trained at Fort Leavenworth after 1956. Vietnamese military schools began to receive U.S. advisers and field manuals. Vietnamese tactics and techniques began to be influenced by American concepts. Up to 1960 however, enemy military activity was insignificant and Vietnamese techniques changed little in practice. Operations conducted to assume control of and pacify areas vacated by Communist troops in accordance with the 1954 Geneva Accords were more political than military. Units had orders to display strength, to win hearts and minds of the people, and to use their weapons only as a last resort. The few military operations that were conducted were opposed by poorly trained, ill-equipped private armies of bandit and religious groups such as the Binh Xuyen in the Rung Sat campaign and the Hoa Hao in the Dinh Tien Hoang and Thoai Ngoc Hau campaigns.

In the meantime, military theory was an area of dispute between two divergent schools of thought in military schools as well as in the training exercises; one being held by officers still under the influence of French practice and previous battlefield experience, the other by those who had been trained in U.S. military schools. The latter began to gain ascendency when the RVNAF began receiving armored personnel carriers and helicopters. The employment of these pieces of equipment necessarily entailed the adoption of U.S. techniques and tactics and the help of U.S. advisers.

Armored personnel transport was not new to RVNAF but heliborne operations constituted a genuinely new dimension in combat. The enemy reacted with surprise and confusion when the RVNAF first used helicopters against him and this reinforced the confidence of Vietnamese leaders in this tactic. Helicopter assaults eclipsed the parachute assault as the tactic of choice in the RVNAF, although between 1945 and 1954, airborne operations produced brilliant results in audacious raids behind enemy lines. Vietnamese airborne units were the most combat-effective in the National Army and had the most fighting experience.

After the treaty of Paris, airborne units continued to play a prominent role as general reserve and strike forces. Even when enemy activities were still weak, paratroopers were used in small operations, most often to rescue outposts or district seats under attacks or pressure. The headquarters of the airborne brigade kept a book containing data on all outposts, district headquarters and key areas throughout the country. Upon receipt of an order for a rescue mission the brigade staff would consult the book and select the most favorable drop zone in the area. Assembly time was 45 minutes after issuance of the order; the unit was usually airborne in C47s an hour later. Normally these missions employed a single company or a company group but rarely battalion task forces. The largest airborne mission was the last one and involved the commitment of two battalions. They jumped east of National Highway 13 in support of the road-clearing mission to resupply Phuoc Long in June 1965.

Two other important developments occurred during the transition from RVNAF and French to American techniques and tactics. First was the effort to secure the railroad from enemy attack; the second was the employment of commando techniques to counter Communist guerrilla activities.

Successful enemy attacks on the railroad not only disrupted transportation but achieved their political goal of demonstrating the erosion of the national authority and the heightened prestige of the Communists. To deal with attacks on trains, a unit called the Railroad Safety Protection Group was activated in 1960. Armored rail cars, called Wickham

An ARVN Airborne Battalion Moves Through Tall Grass
Toward a Bamboo Thicket in Search of the Enemy, 1962

Trolleys, equipped with 37-mm guns, machine guns, radios and searchlights carried reaction forces. Locomotives were preceded by one or more flatcars to detonate mines on the track. These cars were armed with Claymore mines on both sides to kill the enemy in his ambushes. Areas most dangerous as ambush sites were secured before the train moved by road-clearing infantry units. Artillery, helicopters and airplanes supported the security forces. Even with all these preparations and all this assembled firepower, however, a small team of guerrillas, or sometimes a single saboteur, was able to disable a train by one well-placed command-detonated mine.

After 1960 VC guerrillas and local forces became increasingly effective and were able to escape contact before regular ARVN units came onto the scene of an attack or ambush. To deal with this situation, the government of the First Republic introduced commando-type units and techniques. Commando units (rangers) operated in company strength or company group strength and were characterized by light equipment, constant movement (they never remained in one position for more than three days) and readiness to engage any enemy target of opportunity. They raided enemy facilities and training camps, ambushed enemy liaison routes, and conducted deep reconnaissance missions. Rangers were originally dressed in black pajamas, wore rubber sandals, and used Communist weapons. They were distinguished from the enemy only by means of colored handkerchiefs worn on some part of the uniform. When ranger units began to receive training from U.S. Army Special Forces, the black pajamas gave way to mottled camouflage uniforms because the Vietnamese Quartermaster Corps budget no longer included money to buy the appropriate fabric. Rubber sandals yielded to U.S. style combat boots and because weapons captured from the enemy were neither adequate nor of uniform models, because appropriate ammunition was hard to come by, and because the methods of employing them were unfamiliar, ranger units were equipped with the same weapons as ARVN infantry.

The switch to U.S. tactics and techniques occurred progressively between 1954 and 1964, but it was not until U.S. forces were actively involved in combat in 1965 that ARVN tactics were brought firmly into

line with those of the U.S. As U.S. forces gained more experience and
new equipment, techniques and tactical concepts continued to develop;
the RVNAF followed along in these developments.

Modified Tactics and Their Effects

Faced with the tremendous prestige of the U.S. Army's well-organized military establishment, with its solid staff procedures, its tactics and techniques that improved constantly as new weapons and equipment were introduced, the RVNAF yielded to total adoption of U.S. doctrine. In a memorandum issued in 1967, the Joint General Staff instructed military schools and units to adopt U.S. field manuals as official operating procedures, pending the development of new manuals by the RVNAF. That memorandum recognized a *fait accompli*.

American field manuals and military schools were not the prime sources of instruction for ARVN units on U.S. Army methods of operation. Practical experience in the field in close cooperation with American units was the best teacher. In fact, some of the techniques were not yet written down in the manuals or taught in the schools. An example was the *Eagle Flight* operation. Particularly suited to relatively flat and open terrain, the *Eagle Flight* technique employed aerial search to find the enemy, pursuit and fixing of the enemy by gunships, vigorous heliborne assault and rapid withdrawal in order to stage the next operation.

New techniques for road-clearing and counter-ambush operations also were developed. Before 1965 ambushes occurred frequently and rarely failed. Many counter-ambush measures were tried but were largely ineffective. But from 1966 onward, enemy ambushes were sharply reduced. Security and counter-ambush concepts did not change much but the abundant means and fast-moving forces rendered the old measures effective. For instance, observation flights conducted while road convoys were in motion could uncover ambushes and bring new, more powerful artillery and bombing strikes on them much more rapidly than before. Reinforcements could be brought to the fight by helicopter to relieve, reinforce, or block the enemy withdrawal. The ambushed units were more confident and better equipped to defend themselves while waiting for help which they knew would be available immediately.

Reconnaissance patrols were also improved. Formerly reconnaissance patrols had to walk into their objective area and walk out with their reports. Consequently, their range was limited and the information was often stale by the time they returned with their reports. With helicopter transport, reconnaissance teams could conduct long-range forays into enemy sanctuaries and along enemy avenues of infiltration and lines of communication. Combat rations, lighter and more nutritious, also allowed longer missions. Improved signal communications enabled the patrols to maintain contact with helicopters and observation airplanes.

ARVN reconnaissance and combat operations were generally restricted to supporting artillery range. Knowledge of this fact helped the enemy to define ARVN's area of operations and objectives. When helicopters became available to move artillery the enemy could no longer rely with confidence on artillery deployments as indicators of ARVN intentions.

Firepower and helicopter mobility were two factors that greatly influenced tactics and techniques. The enemy became aware of this very quickly and tried to develop countermeasures. For example, he would move rapidly away from helicopter landing zones as soon as the helicopters were sighted or when artillery or air preparations began. We dealt with this enemy reaction by making simulated helicopter assaults on landing zones and making real assaults on other landing zones to trap the enemy fleeing from the simulated landing. This method achieved some results, although it could not be effectively repeated often in one area.

In the Mekong Delta, a tactic appropriate to the intricate system of waterways there involved coordination of riverine units of the Navy with infantry units. The Navy provided fire support and blocked enemy escape while ARVN infantry assaulted from helicopter or was transported to the objective by Navy boats. When helicopters were used these operations were very effective.

Operations such as these were successful only when precise and detailed intelligence was available. Consequently, one of the most regular missions of riverine units was patrolling and searching river traffic for enemy patrols, weapons, ammunition, explosives, and for rice being moved toward enemy sanctuaries. Search operations usually were concentrated on enemy water supply routes but one of the difficulties was the fact that enemy boats were dispersed among the people's boats. A careful search required a great deal of time. Supplies were frequently stashed in double-bottomed boats or tied to the sides of boats for ease of dumping in case of imminent discovery.

Riverine forces also escorted convoys of rice, charcoal and firewood from the western delta to the eastern, especially through sectors where ambushes were frequent. The Hoa Tu River between Bac Lieu and Ba Xuyen, and the Cho Gao Canal from the Bassac River to the Vam Co Rivers were frequent ambush sites.

Riverine operations were only one type of combined operations conducted by RVNAF. Combined operations would frequently involve ARVN units, RF, PF, National Police, and often general reserve units such as paratroopers, marines and rangers. Most operations were supported by artillery, armor, the Air Force or the Navy. But in each case, good results depended greatly on good cooperation between commanders because senior commanders never relinquished full operational control of their subordinate units to commanders of other forces even when the task organization called for it.

The most frequent deficiency in combined operations was that operational commanders tended to assign lighter and less dangerous missions to their own units and the harder ones to attached units. Furthermore, difficulties often arose because task-force units still responded to direction from their parent units, even though attached or under operational control of another unit. One major reason for failure in the defense of Quang Tri in April 1972 was that the ranger and marine brigades and armored groups placed under control of the 3d Infantry Division failed to cooperate with or respond to orders of the 3d Division commander.

Up until 1973, there was only one inter-regional operation. It was in the 3d and 4th Military Regions in 1970 when RVNAF staged the cross-border operation into Cambodia. Military Regions 3 and 4 cooperated effectively again in 1974 in another foray into Cambodia.

The experience of *Operation Lam Son* 719 into Laos in 1971 and in the loss of Quang Tri during the Communist 1972 Summer Offensive revealed inability of I Corps Headquarters to execute corps-level operations. The other corps headquarters were similarly inexperienced and ill-equipped to handle multi-division operations. On the other hand, most ARVN staffs and the appropriate commanders could manage division and lower level operations effectively. In March 1975, the 22d Division in Binh Dinh and the 18th Division in Long Khanh proved the abilities of these two divisions and their commanders against great odds.

When U.S. forces and advisers were still in Vietnam, ARVN major unit staffs were hard to evaluate because of the U.S. help and support they got. A case in point was the Vietnamese 1st Infantry Division, which became more celebrated than any other Vietnamese infantry division. But it was more fortunate than others because at one time each of its regiments received the strongest assistance and support of an American division. As a result, the 1st Division ranked with the Airborne Division and the Marine Division as a crack unit of the RVNAF.

Solving Difficult Tactical Problems

Throughout the Vietnam War, despite the abundant U.S. support and modern tactics, four tactical problems remained not fully solved. Two of them had existed ever since the beginning of the war, and two developed since 1968. The two old problems were how to conduct effective night operations and how to execute succcesful cordon and search operations. The two more recent problems were how to counter enemy sapper actions and to reduce the effectiveness of enemy shelling of the cities and air bases.

The Vietnam war pitted the adversaries against each other in every sense. The opposition existed between ideologies: Free society versus Communism; and between strategies: immediate solution versus long-term struggle; and day versus night actions.

Night Operations

The allies almost invariably conducted offensive operations during the day while nearly all Communist activities took place under starlight. This almost exclusive preference—day for the allies and the enemy for the night—indeed corresponded to the nature of life and activities of the opposing sides. In Communist-controlled areas, all facets of civilian life—commerce, trade, markets—were conducted before dawn and ceased at sunrise when RVNAF began to operate. Enemy units took advantage of darkness to move personnel and supplies; to mount harassment and offensive sabotage actions against outposts, bridges, and roads; to start shelling, to conduct propaganda activities, collect taxes, and carry out assassinations and kidnappings.

Darkness was a Communist tool and it created two important advantages: security and surprise. Security was achieved because of immunity from detection and hence from destruction by air strikes. Surprise was gained because it gave the ability to vanish into the landscape and into the populace, or to emerge unexpectedly from these to initiate offensive action. The Communists became thoroughly familiar with night life and nature whether it was in the jungles, mountains or lowlands; in the swamps, or along the rivers of trails. Guides and liaison agents played important roles in night movement. They were not only familiar with the terrain but also with habits of RVNAF outpost troops and their nightly routines, such as periodic firing schedules.

The RVNAF leadership fully understood the advantages any attacker should be able to exploit in night operations and constantly encouraged ARVN units to execute a greater share of their offensive actions under the cover of darkness. But the ARVN suffered a number of handicaps which degraded the effectiveness of its night operations. One of these was the elusiveness of suitable enemy targets for night attacks. While the enemy could emerge at night from the cover of forests or swamps to attack fixed RVNAF bases and population centers, the ARVN task was just the opposite: to depart from prominent, well-known bases or from conspicuous field operating sites and enter the deep jungles or treacherous swamps in search of an almost invisible enemy.

Secondly, only country people had a natural affinity for night operations. ARVN officers and noncommissioned officers were all urban dwellers. They were chosen for their educational backgrounds, high school graduates were sent to officer candidates' schools and junior high school certificate holders to non-commissioned officers schools. To achieve these degrees, students had to go to schools in district or province capitals. Rural peasants almost never had this opportunity. Even most enlisted men in the National Army were not rural peasants but urbanized peasants and workers who had had contacts with the machine age.

Thirdly, the life and activities of the people on the government side were geared to the day; night was habitually devoted to sleep. The switch from diurnal to noctural activities, though logical, was not easy to make. Furthermore, the scattered posts, manned by squads, platoons and companies, did not have enough people to perform normal duties such as road-clearing and search operations, let alone conduct night operations as well, and when the busy harvest time came around, many PF personnel had to work in the fields during the day; placed on a night ambush position, they would use the time to rest.

From 1967 on, night training became part of the curriculum of military schools, and in general occupied one-fifth of the total training. The training emphasized individual combat and unit training: night firing, bivouacs, ambushes, reconnaissance patrols, offense and defense. The training was conducted in safe areas and not many schools ventured to take trainees to areas with realistic conditions. Furthermore, few instructors of night combat had been selected on the basis of combat experience so there was a lack of confidence in them on the part of trainees.

Personnel assigned routine night duty, from leaders to team members, were chosen for a number of criteria, of which physical fitness was one. Men who coughed or who could not stand the cold damp were filtered out. But those who had already proved their reliability under fire were taken regardless of other considerations.

There was hardly a soldier who had had night combat duty but did not have a memorable story or two. When I was a company commander on a night ambush in 1952 during the war against the Viet Minh in North Vietnam, one of my squad leaders reported by radio that several enemy soldiers were sighted and would be passing through his ambush area. Just then all radio communication ceased. The full story did not come to light until after the sergeant returned the next morning. The enemy was in such strength, of battalion size, that the ambushing unit did not wish to risk engagement, and had to turn its radio off to avoid detection.[1] ARVN ambush units were eventually supplied with the AN/PRC-6 radio set which, if accurately tuned and equipped with fresh batteries, could be operated without the rushing noise by adjusting the squelch knob.

Encounters between ambushing units and enemy battalions were rare. Most of the time contact was made with units of platoon or squad size, liaison teams, escorts, or members of the VCI. For this reason, most ambush units were of platoon or squad size. Their usual weapons were M-16 rifles, M-60 machine guns, M-79 grenade launchers, grenades, and Claymore mines which proved to be most effective. During a night raid on an enemy provincial headquarters in Tuyen Duc in April 1972, a RF company moved into position around the suspected house and placed Claymore mines to cover all exits from the house. Once ready the raiding party gave a deafening cry. The enemy, roused from sleep, scrambled out of the house directly into the paths of the exploding mines. He suffered 20 men killed among whom was a provincial commissar. The raiding company had no casualties..

The U.S. forces employed a number of night techniques such as *Night Hunter* and *Stalker*. RVNAF tried to adopt them, but the *Night Hunter* technique called for a complicated maneuver of at least three elements: a ground radar team, a cavalry element in armed helicopters, and a direct support artillery element. Sometimes there was a fourth element, the reaction force. When the AN/TPS-25 radar station picked up enemy

---

[1] The SCR-536 was then the standard radio set for squads and platoons. Its receiver emitted a loud, constant rushing sound when turned on and had no squelch control.

presence, artillery would deliver air bursts and light up the target with illuminating rounds. The airborne cavalry would close in, strafing. Airmobile infantry would land if the situation warranted. Because *Night Hunter* required excellent communications and coordination in addition to the necessary equipment, RVNAF had great difficulty mustering the resources to conduct these operations.

The *Stalker* technique employed sharpshooters equipped with infrared scopes who would lie in wait in areas likely to be frequented by the enemy. This did not require much complicated equipment but was suitable only to deal with isolated individual movements. The JGS asked MACV to provide training in this technique and a number of soldiers of the 7th Infantry Division at Camp Dong Tam (Dinh Tuong Province) received the training. The technique was not fully exploited however because the Starlight Scope rifle was too heavy for the individual sharpshooter to handle well in the field at night.

The infrequency of night operations remained a long-standing weakness with ARVN units.

Cordon and Search

Cordon and search was a technique to trap and destroy enemy regional units, scattered guerrillas, and VCI members who had entered hamlets to operate or take refuge. Two coordinated operations were involved: cordon the hamlet; then search it.

A cordon was most effective if executed in silence under the cover of darkness. Cordoning units had to have sufficient strength to block likely routes of escape and to defend against any enemy attempt to relieve the hamlet from the outside.

The search unit was organized into teams whose members were thoroughly trained in search techniques. They knew the techniques of caching arms and documents, of digging and using undergound shelters for personnel, and how to avoid mines and booby traps. During the preparation phase, search units were briefed on the target area through diagrams, maps, photographs, and, in some cases, aerial photographs. They had to have a thorough and detailed knowledge of the target and the personnel that they expected to apprehend.

The search was conducted in two steps: an initial search and a thorough search. The initial stage began with a rapid and unexpected entry into the objective, leaving no time for enemy reaction such as hiding materials and weapons, taking cover in secret hideouts, laying mines and booby traps, or launching a counterattack. Entrance into the hamlet would be made from several directions if possible. Once the objective was secured and under control, the thorough search would begin.

The thorough search was conducted methodically. If the hamlet was in a contested area, the people would be interviewed to obtain initial information needed for the search. The calm, alarmed, or anxious attitude of the people being interviewed would indicate whether the targets being sought were present. Children were a reliable source of information because they rarely lied, or if they did, their lies would be transparent. The people were encouraged to reveal the locations of mines and booby traps, but regardless of tipoff, mines and booby traps had to be carefully sought, detected, marked, and neutralized or destroyed.

The people were asked to point out the shelters they had dug for protection against shelling. Usually these underground shelters were dug close to where they slept, such as under the beds. A search started immediately to see if these underground shelters led to underground hideouts.

Inside dwellings, hideouts might have been made in double walls; these could be detected by tapping on the outer walls. Brick houses might have hiding space under the roof. Indoor shelters were usually small, consisting of a froghole type of chamber with an opening barely large enough for one person to squeeze through and with an underground room large enough to allow for movement and to store emergency water and supplies. These holes were covered over with a jar of water, a jar of rice, a chaff pile, or some other customary object.

Supplies and document caches were also searched for in dwellings. Because they were used daily they were likely to be hidden close at hand and where they would be protected from rain. Caches of these supplies were usually found in bamboo sections telescoped together as fake rafters, in hollowed-out and carefully closed house pillars, or in religious altars or ancestors' altars which searchers as a rule would not touch out of reverence. Floors too were good candidates for caches. The most effective way to detect them was to pour water over the dirt floor. Places that had been excavated would absorb more water at a faster rate than those that hadn't. Fireplaces and kitchen hearths were also suspect.

In the yard, hiding places could be in strawstacks and could be detected by pulling bundles of straw from several places. Where the straw concealed hollows, it gave easily on pulling, and this might indicate a hiding place. However, such a hideout was merely temporary and improvised. Other improvised but frequent refuges were in ponds under aquatic vegetables and hyacinths, where the quarry would breathe through a reed allowing him to remain submerged for two or three hours.

Most hiding places were carefully prepared in advance. Some of these were detected by their entrances or ventilation pipes. Entrances were small and covered by boards or sturdy bamboo wattles camouflaged by dirt and grass. They were built in out-of-the-way spots such as bamboo groves, bushes and dense underbrush or in malodorous spots like pigsties. Vents, usually made from bamboo sections, were placed in least suspected places, perhaps under a heap of firewood, under a stone heap, in ponds, wells, or connecting to roof-supporting bamboo pillars, or even camouflaged as clothsline posts.

Group hideouts or those for important cadres were usually elaborate and had sleeping quarters and storage space. Because they were built far below the surface entrance they were reached by tunnels. Tunnels were dug in an intricate network with many exists opening into rice paddies, cemeteries or river banks. Sometimes two kilometers long, tunnels took a great deal of work and secrecy to build and were usually built only in Communist-controlled areas. Here tunnels were usually strong, shored by bamboo wattles, and protected by mines and spikes to slow down and discourage searches. Such sturdily built tunnels usually daunted search parties who, in many instances, used riot control agents to flush out any enemy personnel. One of the difficulties encountered by search parties once inside the tunnels was the difficulty in communicating with the outside and the high probability of becoming lost. A few units tried to follow the progress of search parties by supplying them with signal equipment and having them report their azimuth every time they made a turn.

In government controlled areas, searches were usually conducted in the presence of local authorities and with the participation of local police forces. In contested areas, especially during the period of U.S. participation, searches were conducted in conjunction with psychological warfare action, medical assistance, gift-giving, distribution of clothes, food-stuffs, books, magazines and newspapers. This mode of operation was known as the Hamlet Festival or County Fair. These operations gained wide currency among the Vietnamese units that operated with U.S. forces but fell into disuse after American forces withdrew because the resources needed to conduct them were not available to the RVNAF.

Cordon and search actions continued however. It was difficult to conduct effective cordon and search operations without inciting considerable resentment among the people toward the government. The discontent that the populace already felt when their houses were being subjected to a thorough search would, when aggravated by any inconsiderate act by an individual or team, severely undermine the people's good will toward the government. The problem was that few villagers believed that searching was necessary for their own security and virtually all of them considered it a nuisance and an invasion of their homes.

Defense Against Sappers

Sapper action was a special method of combat which employed a small force to achieve major results. In an address delivered on 19 March 1967 at the Sapper Training School in North Vietnam, located at the headquarters of the 305th Sapper Group, Ho Chi Minh said: "Sapper action is a special action which requires special effort and special skills to perform." This statement was found in the records of every major Communist sapper unit. The Sapper Corps was a special combat arm that was trained to oppose a greater force with lesser strength and to move in complete silence. It was created after the pattern of successful guerrilla units of the Viet Minh and raised to an exceptionally high degree of sophistication. The Sapper Corps originated in 1946 when the Viet Minh imaginatively employed professional thieves with special skills and competencies such as martial arts, swimming, climbing and house-breaking, to penetrate French installations and bases and steal weapons, ammunition, explosives, documents, or carry out assassinations or sabotage.

In 1965 the General Headquarters for the South (COSVN) gave special impetus to the development of Sapper forces with the following objectives in mind:

- To destroy and erode the strength of RVNAF and allied forces.

- To demolish war materiel and strategic and tactical objectives.

- To penetrate and destroy command facilities, outposts, billets, service bases, supply bases, signal centers, radar stations, and military schools.

- To penetrate and strike air bases, airfields, seaports, river boats, military vessels, docks, fire bases, and mechanized bases.

- To penetrate and sabotage defense firms and factories of military value.

- To investigate and conduct battlefield preparation for the infantry, and to secure footholds to pave the way for infantry advance.

- To strike key areas and to act in concert with the infantry in both defense and offense during military campaigns or series of actions.

- To organize against mop-up operation and to mount ambushes and counterambushes.

From 1969 onward, realizing that the commitment of major units to confront the U.S. Army and ARVN was a costly failure, COSVN converted several infantry battalions to sapper battalions and gave sapper training to all infantry units.

There were two kinds of sappers: surface sappers and underwater sappers, and two forms of underwater sapper activities, mining and frogmen's attacks. In the first nine months of 1970, 189 underwater sapper actions were executed. Of the 138 minings in this total, 52 (or 38 percent) were successful. Of the 51 attacks by frogmen, 28 (or 55 percent) were successful. The sappers' most outstanding achievements were the destruction of USS Krishna on 7 August 1970, the VNN ship HQ 225 on 30 July 1970 in An Xuyen, the blowing up of three barges carrying 300 tons of ammunition in the Saigon River on 5 March 1972, and the burning of the Nha Be gasoline depot on 2 December 1973.

The sapper threat was realized and given high priority by security units. Small outposts took inexpensive measures for detecting infiltration, which were nevertheless effective, such as raising dogs, geese, and ducks on the outer perimeter of their positions. However, sappers tried to erase their human scent by lying in the night dew for a long time; then they would calmly walk up to the dogs and stroke their heads and pet them. If chased, they would jump into a mud hole to obliterate the scent and lead the dogs astray. But the crudest countermeasure was to eliminate the dogs with food mixed with a tranquilizer or poison. To deal with geese and ducks, they attached a stalk of blackened waterpotato plant to the end of a walking stick and dangled it upwind in front of the birds. Thinking they saw snakes, the birds did not dare make a sound. Another way they distracted the ducks and geese was to rub green onion leaves on the sappers' bodies. The smell frightened the birds because they thought they smelled vipers.

Mines and booby traps were effective though expensive defenses against sappers. A minefield had to have several kinds of mines, alternately laid; some self-activating mines and some command controlled. Minefields were sometimes strewn with barbs cut from barbed wire. This made it more difficult for the sappers to detect the three-pronged triggers of the mines. Tin cans and noise-making obstacles were rigged to warn sentries. A system of searchlights and armor support near the perimeter of a protected installation also made the sapper's task more difficult but these resources were available only for the most important facilities.

The earthen and concrete bunkers and blockhouses that characterized the outpost and garrison defenses were prime targets for sappers who endeavored to breach them during the assault on the installation. A well placed satchel charge was usually enough to do the job but in order to get close enough to use one, the sappers would have to neutralize the defenders in the bunker with fire or grenades. An effective protection against this sort of assault was a double net of barbed wire in which the meshes were smaller than a grenade. The outer layer protected the entire bunker while the inner one covered the firing ports.

Against underwater sappers, the most common defense for ships consisted of spotlights to illuminate the surface of the water and searchlights to sweep the banks. Another method called for throwing grenades around the ships' hulls, but this was expensive. Among other defenses tried was sinking a high-intensity light in a ball deep below the surface but this proved ineffective since the light did not radiate far enough. Less costly and more effective ways included frequent river patrols on sampans, mine clearing by small craft dragging hooked steel cables, and periodic engine idling to hamper frogmen with the turning propeller.

An effective way to protect bridges was a wire mesh around bridge supports. Wire nets were spread upstream about 100 meters from the bridge on floats to stop drifting mines, frogmen, and especially water hyacinths which were frequently used by sappers for concealment. Troops would fire at approaching hyacinths as a precautionary measure.

Communist sappers who had rallied were employed to stage demonstrations at large bases and major headquarters. At Long Binh Base, one such demonstration showed that sappers could break through the several barbed wire fences in only ten minutes. Demonstrations of bridge mining, of carrying explosives on personnel and on rafts, and methods of remaining under water for extended periods were most effective instruction techniques. In order to reap the most benefit from these demonstrations, in 1973 the JGS General Agency for Military Training sent NCO instructors from Quang Trung Training Center to a sapper course conducted by ex-sappers. These NCOs then toured the military regions holding demonstrations of their own.

Among anti-sapper measures which U.S. forces employed there were some that ARVN could not adopt and had to modify. For example, to combat frogman-sappers at Cam Ranh Base, live electric wire was trailed in the

An Ex-Sapper Demonstrates Infiltrating Through Barbed Wire and a Mine Field at Long Binh, August 1969

water, and dolphins were used as well as U.S. Navy frogmen to detect sappers. These measures were hard for the RVNAF to duplicate for lack of resources. Although the Vietnamese Navy had frogmen, they were few and too ill-equipped for extensive use.

The use of seismic and other mechanical and electronic sensors in the defense of vital bases had to be abandoned after the U.S. withdrawal because the sensors had to be replaced after only a short time in service. When the supply of fresh sensors was exhausted, the RVNAF was not resupplied. In any event, the sensors' effectiveness was rather limited; they were unable to distinguish between people and animals.

U.S. anti-sapper measures were frequently modified by the RVNAF because the resources were not available to adopt the American system in its entirety. The Long Binh Base was a case in point. The U.S. defense had two illumination systems: one to illuminate the inward side of the fence and a system of searchlights to illuminate the outer side. The high grass, being an obstacle to observation, was killed by herbicides. When the Long Binh Base was turned over to ARVN, grass became a problem because the RVNAF had no herbicide or efficient mowing equipment. The far-reaching beacon-lights were no longer available. The base defense forces had to revise the security plan. Lights were now beamed on the inside of the fence only. The wire mesh perimeter fence was replaced by a sheet iron fence painted white because experience had shown that wire mesh fences were more easily cut than sheet iron fences. The white paint aided in detecting breaches in the fence. Because grass became uncontollable, a concrete path was laid around the perimeter. Troops were issued bicycles to replace the motor vehicles of earlier times. The advantage achieved was complete silence without sacrificing much speed.

The defense of U.S.-transferred bases ran into the dual problem of reduced resources and personnel shortages. Bases that had been built for divisions were defended by units no larger than a RF battalion. Penetration into such bases was easy for sappers, but since they no longer housed headquarters and supplies, they lost their attractiveness as targets.

In summary, enemy sapper action was a very effective tactic in the war of attrition and annihilation in terms of material damage and psychological and propaganda impact. The success of sapper action depended on courage, cleverness and resourcefulness.

Anti-sapper action had to be based on continuous vigilance, elimination of routine patterns, and most important, cleverness and resourcefulness to combat the enemy's cleverness and resourcefulness.

Defense Against Shelling

Shelling was the most frequent Communist tactic. They used it extensively in guerrilla as well as conventional operations. Shelling was appropriate in guerrilla actions because it harassed and exhausted the enemy, and fought more with less.

When in 1968 Communist forces began to be equipped with artillery rockets and several kinds of field artillery, preparation shelling was used before infantry assaults. The tactic of "first shelling, then assault" became routine after that time. For a number of enemy military leaders, artillery was a substitute for the air power which they could not employ in the South. In battles such as that of Quang Tri during the 1972 summer offensive, the enemy's 130-mm artillery was so successful in pounding ARVN outposts in the DMZ that defensive troops were pinned down while enemy infantry was closing in with impunity.

Such large-scale utilization of artillery occurred only in large engagements, but sporadic shelling occurred everywhere. This kind of shelling was often conducted by three-man teams with artillery rockets or a single mortar. The targets were usually small posts, garrisons or villages and were easy to hit with a few rounds. The effect on the people in the target area was often greatly out of proportion to the number of rounds fired or the damage inflicted. It was a matter of personal survival to them, while a 1,000 round concentration of fire on a remote ARVN unit was just something they might read about in the paper. Take the first rocket shelling on 19 March 1968 against Saigon: a total of 22 rockets fell in the center of the city causing 150 houses to burn, three policemen and two civilians were killed and 32 people were wounded. After this incident, shelling became virtually the only topic of conversation among the population. Materials for the construction of shelters — sandbags and sand — rose sharply in price, then disappeared from the market and the press demanded that government take immediate measures to protect the population from shelling.

A shelling security belt was devised for Saigon and other important cities. This belt was to reach beyond the effective range of rockets, from 8 to 10 kilometers. (Though subsequently Communist troops used booster charges to reach a range of 18 kilometers. With this extended capability, enemy rockets were able to hit Da Nang air base from the foot of the mountains at Hai Van Pass).

Airports, frequent targets of shelling, were usually sited on the outskirts of major cities, about four to five kilometers from the city center. In planning a security belt, the safety zone could not start from the geographical center of the city but from the most outlying targets and often encompassed a radius of about 15 kilometers or more. The area included in this radius was therefore extensive.

Rockets were easy to smuggle in, to conceal, and to fire. They were usually transported to the firing sites days before, concealed underwater in rice paddies or camouflaged. Launching ramps were simple; they could be two logs tied together at one end or small dirt ramps. They were very inaccurate but the objective of the firing was terror rather than military destruction so that did not matter to the enemy.

In cities such as Saigon and Da Nang special task forces were formed to handle defense against shelling. The units involved included ARVN regulars, allied forces, RF, and PF units. The safety zone was divided into areas of responsibility. Units conducted patrols in their assigned areas and set day and night ambushes. Curfews were imposed in the most sensitive areas to avoid confusion and friendly casualties.

The Air Force played an important role in reconnaissance in the security zones and in the detection and attack of firing sites. As soon as night fell, illumination aircraft went aloft to light up suspected routes to firing sites. Helicopters operated in groups of three, one equipped with searchlights and the other two armed to strike suspected targets while artillery provided the main counterbattery fire. Artillery observers manned observation posts closest to the anti-shelling security belt. They were equipped with radars to detect firings but the effective range of these radars was limited to about three kilometers. Areas uncovered by radar were protected by ambushes and minefields. Each night the Saigon anti-shelling task force set as many as 100 ambushes around the city. Some radars were teamed with sensor fields but this technique lasted only while the U.S. was still providing the sensors.

In 1967, Danang authorities constructed a bamboo fence several kilometers long protected by a series of small guardposts but the enemy found it relatively easy to breach. Furthermore, the peasants in the area found it inconvenient and broke it in many places. The project was eventually scrapped.

For all their deficiencies, the measures worked out and implemented by the task forces were as effective as could be expected. Take, for example, the case of Saigon City. From late May to late June 1968, the enemy shelled Saigon eight times. After the task force began to work, the enemy was unable to launch another shelling until mid-August and only two additional until the end of that year.

Patrols in the security belt proved effective in capturing rockets that had not been used, and in preventing transportation of additional rockets from enemy bases into the security zone. In mid September 1968, an ARVN unit captured a battery of 12 tubes of 107-mm rockets in Can Giuoc, Long An Province, south of Saigon. Effective patrolling also caused the enemy to delay firings. A number of rockets, buried too long, failed to explode on impact. In shelling of Saigon on 31 October 1968, four out of eight rockets fired were duds. All units, however, did not perform their patrol duties with zeal or integrity. There was the time when the enemy firing position was in the ambush site supposedly occupied by friendly troops. An investigation revealed that the RVNAF unit had neglected, out of laziness, to move far enough and had instead set up a kilometer short of its objective. After this, commanders were punished when the enemy succeeded in firing from the commander's sector of responsibility. Cash awards were given to units that captured rockets or caught shelling teams in ambush. Eight rockets were once captured in Tan Uyen

District, Bien Hoa Province. A patrol uncovered the battery of 122-mm rockets timed to go off by a clockwork. Other similar instances of capture occurred, such as where rockets were timed to fire by ingenious mechanical timers. These instances showed that enemy shelling teams were afraid of discovery and counterbattery fire.

Sometimes the enemy took advantage of RVNAF negligent habits to time their shelling. Many shellings occurred between 5:30 and 6:30 in the morning. After some investigation and study, the task force discovered that VNAF patrol aircraft stopped operations and landed before dawn, assuming that the enemy would not risk shelling at daybreak. Such errors of judgment were studied and quickly exploited by the enemy.

Besides the military measures described above, pacification measures contributed to the tactical effort to counter enemy shelling. The pacification effort was intensified in the areas adjoining the rocket belt. Organizations associated with this effort, such as the police, revolutionary development cadres, and self-defense militia, were mobilized to gather information concerning enemy shelling activities. The effectiveness of pacification measures was such that the enemy was forced to plan his shellings as elaborately as any other military operation, employing security forces, rocket transportation units, and other resources. As more units became involved, the operations became easier for RVNAF to discover and prevent. Many attempts were aborted through the combined investigation and intelligence effort of U.S. and Vietnamese forces. Nevertheless it was easier for the enemy to shell than it was for RVNAF to prevent it and counteraction required many resources, much coordination, and great determination. When these were mustered in sufficient degree to minimize the shelling threat, the RVNAF forces involved tended to lose the initiative for other operations, they exhausted resources needed for other high-priority tasks, and became tied to the defense of a limited area.

CHAPTER VI

Special U.S. Combat Techniques

United States forces found that the tactics and techniques that were generally employed during World War II and the Korean War were largely inadequate to cope with the battlefield conditions they found in Vietnam. Furthermore, the Vietnam War presented the American military leadership with opportunities to develop new weapons and devices, and to test concepts of employment of equipment designed after the end of World War II. The wide use of helicopters, for example, spawned numerous new applications of these versatile machines. The more routine of these applications, such as battlefield reconnaissance, command and control, combat assault, logistic support and medical evacuation were gradually adopted by RVNAF as the equipment became available, but other more sophisticated applications remained exclusively in the U.S. arsenal. Examples of these were helicopters specially equipped with night vision and illumination devices and odor detecting *People-sniffer* equipment. The VNAF was equipped with gunships for the support of ground troops but these were the familiar *Huey* helicopters and not the more modern *Cobras* introduced by the U.S. Army later in the war.

With minor exceptions, such as those mentioned, modern American equipment, and the tactics and techniques developed by the U.S. Army and Air Force for the employment of that equipment were gradually transferred to the RVNAF.

Besides the extensive use of helicopters in virtually every possible military application, four other major battlefield techniques were developed to a high degree of expertise by the Americans in

Vietnam. The most prominent of these was the employment of massed B-52 strategic bombers in a tactical role. Heavy bombers had been used in support of ground operations in World War II and Korea but never on the scale they were employed in Vietnam. As used in South Vietnam, these heavy bombers were the most destructive of all weapons and the psychological and political effects of their strikes were great.

Second only to the B-52s in the psychological and political repercussions caused was the use of defoliants to eliminate the enemy's concealment in the jungles of Vietnam and his food crops in remote areas.

Closely related to the use of chemical defoliants, but lacking the political and psychological effects, was the employment of huge crawler tractors— *Rome plows*—to remove vegetation that could hide enemy activities.

Finally, chemical warfare (not involving the use of lethal agents as in World War I but incapacitating types of tear gas) made its appearance on the battlefields of Vietnam and also caused some adverse political reactions.

B-52 Bombers

On 18 June 1965, a news report on the war situation in Vietnam commanded the special attention of war watchers. For the first time B-52 bombers were committed to bomb in War Zone D, forty miles northeast of Saigon. The people of Bien Hoa, the province capital on the southern fringe of War Zone D, were stunned by the violent vibrations and series of explosions and woke up to discover a new word: "B-52." It was rumored that no living thing, large or small, in an area hit by B-52s, could survive.

Vietnamese Army troops first looked upon the B-52 strikes as a curious American phenomenon but later learned to appreciate their tremendous destructive effects. This appreciation grew into a feeling of confidence; if the B-52s were in support, all would be well for the ARVN units.

ARVN commanders, however, even at division and corps level, were told very little by the Americans about the techniques of employment of the B-52s. These commanders were consulted during the target selection process and were notified by MACV which targets had been approved, but they were never told the exact time the target would be struck. This practice obviously reflected the Americans' concern for security, for it was not long after the B-52s came to be employed with frequency that we began to hear that the enemy was claiming that he had advance warning about specific B-52 strikes.

The enemy was faced with a serious morale problem. The nearly silent approach of the horrendous violence carried by the B-52s was creating great anxiety among his troops. Defectors and prisoners of war attested to this frequently. They told of the sudden destruction of an entire battalion and once even of a complete regiment. Tunnels and caves collapsed and buried the soldiers alive. There was no escape from the power of these heavy bombs; even near misses would cause internal hemorrhages.

In July 1967 Hanoi Radio announced the death of General Nguyen Chi Thanh, commander of all Viet Cong forces in the South. A report spread throughout the Communist ranks that General Thanh had been killed in a B-52 raid on the Tay Ninh-Cambodia border. This was probably a true report, but its validity didn't matter; it was enough that the troops believed it. The fear of the B-52 spread throughout the Viet Cong ranks like a wave. The high command had to do something to restore confidence and they elected to try to convince the troops that their leaders had prior warning of all strikes in sufficient time to take adequate cover or to vacate the target area.

Soon after COSVN began this internal propaganda effort, prisoners of war and defectors began telling their interrogators that they were warned of impending strikes. Some Americans put too much credence in these reports and assumed that there must be enemy agents in the ARVN staff structure who were passing the information to COSVN. The trouble with this assumption, however, was that few ARVN personnel were informed in advance of all the specifics concerning strikes.

There is a little doubt, however, that the enemy did develop an early warning system of sorts. How effective it could have been is open to serious question, but by piecing together information collected from their available sources, this system might have given some general warning of a B-52 raid on the way.

The enemy learned from experience that U.S. forces often exploited the effects of B-52 strikes, so one indication of an impending strike was preparations for an operation made by American units. Information of this sort wasn't too difficult to collect, but it was not likely to give much of an indication about when and where a B-52 strike might take place.

A more precise source of information about the timing of a B-52 attack was probably the warning given by Soviet intelligence ships believed to be in the waters around the USAF B-52 bases. This sort of information could have been passed to COSVN as well as to Hanoi by radio in time to inform at least some of the Communist troop commands that a flight of B-52s had taken off and were headed to North or South Vietnam.

More precision about where and when the strike would hit was probably gained by monitoring the U.S. commands' artillery advisory radio net. It was standard practice for a warning of "heavy artillery" to be broadcast on this net just prior to a strike. If, in conjunction with this warning the Viet Cong or NVA unit would notice that all American air activity had ceased in its area—the spotter-planes had left and the helicopters they normally saw and heard were absent— they might have good reason to expect a B-52 attack. About this time, since it was now very quiet in the jungle hide-out, the soldiers might hear the faint rumble of the high-flying bombers. If a warning had not already been passed to the troops, it was probably too late by now. Nevertheless, warnings of strikes were frequently given to the troops. If the predicted strike failed to materialize no soldier would be likely to complain. If the strike did happen and some lucky evasive action to avoid destruction had been taken by the unit after the warning, the cadre could take the credit, boast of the great early warning system, and morale would improve.

Although ARVN soldiers came to be very fond of (and possibly too dependent upon) B-52s, the RVNAF leadership and the general population of South Vietnam had some misgivings about B-52s striking close to populated areas. What would happen, many wondered, if by some technical error the bombs fell on a village or if one of the giant bombers itself crashed into a populated area? This concern was natural because the people had seen the effects of errors made by tactical bombers; and the aviators in these planes could see their targets. If they could make such tragic mistakes from such low levels, how could the fliers in the high altitude bombers do any better?

There were a few serious mistakes made by B-52s. The first one was in the That Son region of Chau Doc Province when several bombs impacted in a village. In 1968 a B-52 bomb fell on the edge of a district capital. Generally speaking, however, the B-52 safety record was excellent. It was an accurate system and a safety margin of 3,000 meters on the flank of a target box was usually adequate.

B-52 employment techniques improved over time. Initially, all targets had to be preplanned; no targets of opportunity could be hit. From about mid 1966, however, the USAF developed the capability of switching to alternate targets while in flight. From 1967 on, the great bombers gave close support to infantry units in contact. Missions of this type accounted for about 10 percent of all missions flown.

The B-52 really proved its worth as a close support weapon during the 1972 Communist offensive. An Loc and the ARVN units defending it were saved by the timely and accurate B-52 attacks on the three enemy divisions laying siege to the town. The precision with which the B-52s struck on the northern edge of An Loc undoubtedly saved the 81st Airborne Rangers from being overrun in that sector.

After years of fruitless discussions, North Vietnam's agreement finally to accept the terms of the 1973 cease-fire has been attributed by many as a direct result of the heavy B-52 strikes against North

Vietnam in December 1972. There is little doubt that these devastating air-raids were an important factor in the Communists' decision.

One half hour before the Paris Treaty became effective in South Vietnam—0800 on 28 January 1973—the last B-52 mission was flown against enemy units on the Cua Viet line where the last major battle of the war had taken place between the South Vietnamese Marines and the NVA 325th Division. This strike ended the nine-year involvement of the B-52s in the Vietnam War, and coming as it did in the last minutes before cease-fire, illustrated the fondness for and reliance on the great bombers that had developed over the years among the RVNAF commanders.

Some critics have observed that B-52s, as they were employed in South Vietnam, were a wasteful, wanton exercise in overkill. There is no doubt that it was an expensive weapons system to employ with such frequency against often allusive and indistinct targets. Vo Nguyen Giap, hardly an objective commentator, said that the use of such strategic bombers in a war that had no terrain objectives—a people's war—was a fruitless undertaking.

Putting aside the question of cost—for after all, how can a price-tag be placed on the survival or defeat of a nation—is there any question that the employment of B-52s in support of the ground war in South Vietnam was a successful tactic? I think not. There is little doubt in the minds of senior South Vietnamese military leaders that had B-52s been used during the battle for Phuoc Long in December 1974, the success at An Loc in 1972 would have been repeated. The two NVA divisions that converged on the outnumbered, outgunned little garrison at Song Be-Phuoc Binh would have presented lucrative, massed targets for destruction by B-52s. Had B-52s been used in Phuoc Long, the enemy would not have gone ahead with his plans to attack Ban Me Thuot with three divisions and Darlac would not have fallen. The entire chain of events that led to the defeats and evacuation of Military Regions 1 and 2 would have been averted.

Their pleas for B-52 support in the hour of peril unheeded, South Vietnamese leaders——with the technical assistance of a few Americans brought in for the purpose——had clusters of 32 bombs improvised and dropped on enemy units in Tay Ninh Province, hoping to cause the enemy to believe that the B-52s had returned. They caused violent explosions and fires, but did not save Tay Ninh. Such were the flickering flames of a dying lamp.

Defoliation

Defoliation was introduced into the Vietnam War at the end of 1960. This was the time when Communist military activities in the South had begun to intensify. Each passing day saw more snippings, minings, ambushes, and assaults on outposts. Most of these incidents occurred in areas where dense vegetation provided excellent concealment for the enemy.

Also during this period, the Communist began to reorganize their bases where they grew rice and vegetables for their troops. ARVN operations into enemy zones such as the famed Do Xa Zone in Military Region 2 uncovered vast farms but the ARVN units had no way to destroy the crops. In consultation with U.S. advisors, South Vietnamese military leaders then in 1959 conceived a plan for employing chemical defoliants for this purpose. The U.S. supplied the chemicals and the delivery means.

Until 1965 defoliation was largely unnoticed although the National Liberation Front protested for the first time in 1963. When U.S. forces began participating in combat operations in 1965, defoliation increased by leaps and bounds, partly because of the need to establish new military bases and airfields in densely vegetated areas.

Defoliation became a household word in Vietnamese homes in Saigon and neighboring provinces for the first time in July 1965 when defoliants were used to clear the Long Binh area which was to be the home of U.S. Army, Vietnam, and U.S. II Field Force. Unfortunately, the defoliants sprayed on the brushlands at Long Binh drifted over to the plantations, orchards and farms of Bien Hoa and neighboring Lai Thieu and took a heavy toll of the rich crops of custard-apple, mango, jackfruit, pineapple and other fruits. The effects appeared overnight. Fruit fell from the trees and the rubber trees in the large nearby plantations turned brown and lost their leaves. The people were stunned by the results but didn't know at the time what had caused such devastation. When they finally learned about the defoliants they became worried lest the chemicals also be dangerous to human and animal life. They remained skeptical of the government's explication even after a member of the government's panel at a press conference tasted the defoliation agent. The farmers, worried about ruined crops and bankruptcy were not much comforted by the official word that the effects would not last for more than a year. The government had to establish boards chaired by the provincial agricultural directors to assess damages and set compensation for the farmers.

From then on defoliation became a source of constant anxiety for the growers. In 1966 and 1967, the births of a number of defective babies in Saigon and Tay Ninh were blamed by many people on the defoliants.

In an experiment in 1961, defoliants were issued to VNAF and tried out on jungles. It was discovered that the agents were as effective against jungles as they were against crops and bushland. Soon afterwards, defoliation was carried out to remove vegetation from the roadsides along lines of communication throughout the country, to uncover infiltration routes from sourthern Laos into the 1st and 2nd Military Regions, as well as to wipe out the enemy's crops. The latter effort was part of the plan to deny the enemy his food supply in conjunction with the Strategic Hamlet program which was then being extensively implemented.

The Vietnamese Air Force was incapable of executing the expanding defoliation program so the USAF took over many of the missions. In 1962 about 5,000 hectares of jungle and 700 hectares of farmland were defoliated but the need for defoliation kept increasing day by day: to uncover enemy infiltration routes, lines of communication, storage areas; to destroy crops in enemy-controlled territory; to increase security for water and land transportation networks, and to clear land for critical installations of U.S. and allied forces.

To minimize civilian opposition, procedures were laid down in January 1966 whereby province and district chiefs, with the concurrence of their U.S. advisers, were vested with authority to recommend defoliation in their respective jurisdictions. If the target areas were under Communist control, the officials had to promise to inform the people living there of the reason for defoliation and to help them relocate in government controlled areas if they so elected. In government controlled areas, if the need for defoliation arose for the security of lines of communication or of bases, the officials had to pledge compensation for any affected crops. To speed up compensation, any claims amounting to under 100,000 piasters were handled at the provincial level; larger claims had to be referred to Saigon. Funding was included in the budget of the General Agency for Political Warfare under the rubric of the Civil-Military Spirit fund.

Proposals for defoliation, approved by both Vietnamese and U.S. officials at the local level were submitted through RVNAF channels and eventually had to be approved by MACV and the U.S. ambassador. The government of Vietnam approved no defoliation with crop-destructive effects in the IV Corps area, the rice basket of the South. Crop destruction missions would be approved for the I, II, and III Corps areas if the purpose was to deny the enemy and his sympathizers food, forcing them to devote more manpower to farming and less to military activities. Well-intentioned as it might have been, this exclusion of most of the Mekong Delta from crop-destruction missions was illogical and inappropriate. A case in point was the way the exclusion operated in Dinh Tuong Province, Military Region 4, where the enemy's farming and military activities were consistently more extensive than they were in Long An Province, Military Region 3, where the exclusion did not apply. An even more serious effect of this discrimination showed up in the Central Highlands of Military Region 2. Because there were no absolute bars against crop destruction there, local officials ignored the vulnerability of the Montagnard farms to defoliants used in the jungles. Consequently, many of the farms of these semi-migrant people were destroyed. This exacerbated the general ill-feeling of the Montagnards toward the government and was exploited by the Communists to good effect. The disaffection generated was one of the main reasons behind the Montagnard separatist movement.

The attitude of some of our local officials was not calculated to win the hearts and minds of the people. Some of them would tell their people that if they wanted to be spared the effects of defoliation, they either had to rid themselves of the enemy, or had to leave their homes to settle in government controlled areas. This "take it or leave it" line was not only unfair but counterproductive. How could the people chase the enemy from their areas?

The crop destruction projects were measured in terms of the number of hectares of defoliated land. But the real effects were harder to measure. What were the effects on the people who happened to have to farm in land controlled by the enemy? (They were usually allowed to keep their harvests after paying taxes to the Communists.) Should they have been denied by defoliants the means to survive? Enemy taxation in money, rice, or other crops did not only take place in enemy-controlled territory but also in contested areas and even in areas considered under government control. The Communists collected most of their rice and money in Military Region 4 where no crop destruction was done while the farmers in the other regions, many of whom worked marginal land at best, suffered most from the crop destruction projects.

In the final analysis, the crop interdiction program, although it affected the enemy's food supply to the point of creating shortages in a few units, had only short-lived effects. Units in short supply were resupplied by rear base service troops with rice from Cambodia, the Mekong Delta, or if they were in Military Region 1, from North Vietnam.

Crop destruction by defoliation thus caused popular opposition to the government without any demonstrable advantage; this opposition far eclipsed any real military gain. This fact was eventually recognized by MACV and the government and from 1971 on, defoliation of crops was prohibited.

Defoliation of jungled areas was a different matter. Several dense areas which had been enemy bases for many years no longer provided him sufficient concealment. One such region was the Rung Sat, the delta of the Saigon River through which all ocean-going vessels had to pass to reach the port of Saigon. Defoliated in 1968, this dense mangrove swamp was turned bare for easy observation. It ceased to be dangerous except for infrequent mining incidents. Seven years after defoliation the forest showed no sign of revival.

In many formerly dense areas that had been hit by defoliants, enemy activity sharply decreased because of the exposure. Ambushes and minings along lines of communication abruptly decreased after dense vegetation had been killed by herbicides. Military bases enjoyed greater security as defensive belts were cleared. Defoliants were spread by helicopter in these belts to reduce contamination of adjacent areas.

Defoliants continued in use even after the 1973 cease-fire; the South Vietnamese defense budget for 1973 included one billion piasters for this purpose but only 300 million were actually disbursed. But the agents were used exclusively for clearing brush and jungle for security around bases and along rights-of-way.

The Rome Plow

Few in Vietnam ever heard the term *Rome Plow*. For the few Vietnamese who were familiar with U.S. military activities, the term initially conjured up the image of some secret device or weapon rather than that of a bulldozer equipped with a special blade manufactured by Rome Caterpillar Company of Rome, Georgia.

In a war where the defense was based on a network of fortifications, terrain clearing was a constant requirement. Chemical defoliants weren't available for the small posts; they did the clearing by hand with shovels, hoes and machetes. Occasionally, if they had the excess fuel, they would burn brush with gasoline or fuel oil.

Larger bases could sometimes afford to use mechanized equipment to clear brush from their perimeters. In 1961 the Thu Duc Reserve Officers' Training School, despite its proximity to Saigon, was harassed by small bands of guerrillas who hid in the nearby woods. The best way to eliminate this constant harassment was to remove the woods. The school lacked the resources of its own for such an undertaking but the commandant took advantage of the presence of an engineer company that was building a firing range for the school, borrowed additional civilian bulldozers and cut a road through the woods which was later to be joined by other intersecting roads. This made it possible to run patrols and set ambushes in the woods which diminished enemy guerrilla activities.

In 1966 *Rome Plows* were first tested by American units to clear jungles, to build helicopter landing zones in wooded areas, and to clear sites for military bases. When they were employed in Cu Chi to clear sites for the U.S. 25th Division, *Rome Plows* won the admiration of Vietnamese logistical and engineer units. Trees three feet in diameter were easily sliced through. No trees could fall on the operators who were protected by overhead "headache bars." Old, sturdy bamboo clumps were cleanly cut and uprooted by the blades. Underground rooms and tunnels that had been concealed in dense vegetation were uncovered and destroyed by the bulldozers. Small mines and spiked traps were no obstacles for these mighty machines.

In the first two days of Operation Cedar Falls in the Iron Triangle in 1967, *Rome Plows* cleared three kilometers of 50-meter wide roads. After a month and a half of work, 2,700 hectares were cleared, including 60- to 100-meter wide strips on both sides of the main roads in the Iron Triangle.

Another noteworthy accomplishment of *Rome Plows* was the clearing of National Highway 13 from Lai Khe to Binh Long in the 3rd Military Region. This section had been closed and was not reopened until November 1967, when, during Operation Shenandoah II, *Rome Plows*

Rome Plows Clearing Brush and Leveling Terrain, 1970

cleared 200-meter wide strips of jungle growth from both sides of the highway.

The 1970 Cambodian invasion in the Fishook area showed the efficiency of *Rome Plows* in finding and demolishing enemy underground shelters and tunnels. These results led to the activation in late 1970 of the first of three ARVN ground-clearing companies which became operational in 1971. These companies were employed by platoons in support of divisional pacification operations.

In III Corps, *Rome Plows* were employed to clear dense growth at the main ammunition depot at Thanh Tuy Ha and to build a new road connecting Thanh Tuy Ha to Nhon Trach.

Units in combat operations liked to have the support of *Rome Plows* to destroy booby traps and detonate mines. Only anti-tank mines could damage *Rome Plows*; smaller mines were ineffectual. Since *Rome Plows* were vulnerable to enemy infantry with anti-tank grenades (B-40 and B-41), they had to be protected by infantry. The two problems with *Rome Plows* were their huge consumption of diesel fuel (about 600 gallons a day), and the heavy maintenance service required to keep them running. Fuel resupply proved to be the major problem in fast-moving operations. As for maintenance and repair, Vietnamese ground-clearing companies were plagued by a constant shortage of spare parts. After the U.S. withdrawal, the parts problem became even more serious and the number of serviceable *Rome Plows* dwindled gradually. Nevertheless, through heroic efforts, the RVNAF managed to keep some of the machines in service.

In March 1973, the Vietnamese 3d Infantry Division conducted pacification operations in the Loc Hiep and Go Noi areas of Quang Nam Province, where enemy guerrillas and regional forces were particularly numerous and strong. Supporting these operations was the ground-clearing company of I Corps. The area of operations was covered by thick vegetation and the mines and booby traps were numerous. After three months of operation, *Rome Plows* cleared about 80 square kilometers in the Loc Hiep area, and about 30 square kilometers in the Go Noi area. Underground shelters and tunnels were caved in and filled.

The clearing so changed the face of the land that, according to a captured guerrilla, the enemy was confused and disoriented when he occasionally returned there; familiar landmarks had completely disappeared. This change prompted the 3d Infantry Division to dub the ground-clearing operation "the landmark metamorphosis technique."

When this action was over, however, the clearing company had only seven or eight serviceable bulldozers out of the fifteen available at the beginning. Two or three machines were heavily damaged by anti-tank mines and the remaining were out of commission for lack of spare parts.

We learned that *Rome Plows* were best employed in mass in order to complete the task quickly. This permitted the enemy little opportunity to react and released the security forces quickly for action elsewhere. Also, for long-lasting effect, trees had to be uprooted; when the trunks were only broken they often started growing back again after a while.

Rome Plows did not generate as much opposition as defoliation since their effects were precisely confined and damage to crops and property in the area being cleared was compensated for by the government. Nevertheless, there were demonstrations by people who demanded compensation for property damage in the Phu Cat, Binh Dinh area, where an Air Force base was built. The problem with damage compensation was in fact that the damage compensation schedules were fixed by a law that dated back to French rule and had been changed only once during the First Republic. The failure to bring compensation up to date and to allow for inflation engendered opposition which was unresolvable so long as the legislation remained unchanged.

Another problem was the fact that it was not always easy to determine whether the complaints were legitimate. The difficulty in determining real victims and the payment of compensation to the wrong parties resulted in lawsuits that dragged out for years in Binh Dinh.

Riot Control Agents

Among the weapons employed during the Vietnam War, riot control agents were the only ones that were used on the civilian populace before they were used on the enemy. To control the Buddhist demonstrations in 1963, President Diem's government authorized the use of tear gas grenades for the first time. The people of Saigon became very familiar with these agents.

Riot control agents made their debut in combat operations in 1964 when they were employed by ARVN troops in an attempt to free U.S. prisoners of war held in An Xuyen Province. From then on the tactical employment of riot control agents increased and, after the initial adverse reaction from the foreign press in 1965, the reporters paid less and less attention to it.

In combat operations, tear gas was introduced into underground hideouts and tunnels. Before being supplied this chemical irritant, ARVN troops confronted with underground hideouts during search operations used the old-fashioned technique of smoking-out the occupants. The technique worked fairly well for underground rooms but against tunnels it merely exposed other entrances or vents as the smoke billowed from them.

To counter the smoke, Communist troops maintained a supply of water in their underground shelters. When the smoke entered, they covered their faces with wet towels. Against the chemical agents, lime juice squeezed into wet towels had the effect of reducing tearing. Communist troops were also issued plastic gas masks but they were not very effective. Many prisoners of war said that when hit by tear gas they were nauseated, their heads ached, their eyes and noses started running and their eyes were unable to open for fifteen minutes, during which time they were unable to react to the attack.

Tear gas also proved to be effective in city fighting. In 1968 in the Saigon-Cholon metropolitan area, during which riot control agents were used against the enemy, he suffered a distinct disadvantage because he had no gas masks. He had to give up positions he had meant to hold when confronted with the advance of masked ARVN troops.

Dense concentrations of tear gas were used to deny the use of base areas and routes for a long period of time. The technique employed 55-gallon drums dropped from aircraft and fuzed to burst on contact or close to the ground. This technique was also used to make it difficult for enemy anti-aircraft gunners to fire at low-flying, defoliant-spraying aircraft.

There is no doubt that the sophisticated weapons systems and the new methods of employing the more ordinary weapons and equipment introduced into the Vietnam War by the Americans gave the American forces and the RVNAF some needed advantages over the enemy. While the U.S. was still in the war, these new techniques could be used to great effect by the RVNAF. When the U.S. forces left the scene and American military assistance funds diminished drastically, the advantages RVNAF enjoyed by virtue of its sharing in these American combat techniques disappeared and even turned into disadvantages.

The RVNAF had hundreds of helicopters and sophisticated airplanes but the supplies of spare parts and the fuel to operate them dried up.

The B-52s were no longer there to rescue beleaguered units, and these units had come to rely too heavily on this support.

The government budget could not support a large defoliation program even if one were deemed necessary, and the *Rome Plows* were idled waiting for parts RVNAF could not afford.

In short, the RVNAF had to return to simpler, less costly methods for fighting the war, and success in fighting a defensive war for survival against an aggressive, dedicated enemy requires decisive strategic or tactical advantages. The RVNAF no longer enjoyed the advantages provided by American combat power, and could not afford to provide them for themselves.

CHAPTER VII

Strategies and Tactics of North Vietnam

The military strategy of North Vietnam was part and parcel of her political strategy: no matter how high and widespread the level of violence, the war was only an extension of politics. Though at times the military solution seemed to be pursued at the expense of the political, this predominance was only temporary; the military strategy formed an integral part of the overall political plan.

Since the general strategy of North Vietnam was based on Marxism-Leninism, her military policy had the same basis, and was further influenced by the theory of people's war and experience gained in the successful drive for political power on the mainland by the Chinese Communists.

North Vietnam's strategy was built on the following key points:

(1) Rely principally on the people's strength to build mass political power. Since the people live everywhere, a successful program to win their hearts and minds and to train them and guide them in the forms of the struggle will surely generate tremendous strength in all localities. For this reason, the North acted on the proposition that armed propaganda surpassed military action in importance.

(2) Recognize the importance of rural areas. To build solid bases and rear areas is essential to success. In the Communist conception the rural areas included jungles and mountains. These areas were important because the rugged terrain and the cover they afforded tended to diminish the superior technology of the United States. Furthermore, these areas were inhabited by ethnic minorities whose allegiance, if won to the Communist side, would be detrimental to the GVN.

In this strategy, the Communists were abbetted by the government authorities who often proved to be inept and corrupt. Jungled and mountainous areas were stepping stones in the conquest of the lowlands. Lowlands owed their importance to the fact that they were the locus of human, natural and material resources which both sides struggled to control. Consequently, the countryside became the vital strategic area. Control of rural areas paved the way for establishing bases and facilities in the urban areas. Urban areas were the nerve centers of the Republic of Vietnam, of its political, military, economic and cultural life, where government had the strength it lacked in the rural areas. It was therefore necessary to enter the urban areas, to seize every opportunity to strike the enemy in his own territory, in every way possible, transforming the rear into the frontline and creating a psychology of insecurity in the Republic.

(3) Always maintain the offensive in order to insure strong protection to base and rear areas, to enlarge them, and to carry the war to the enemy's rear. The rear is the key resource that supports the frontline.

These were the three strategic canons of North Vietnam. They were the basic principles of the military policy which was referred to as the *Military Art*.

The Military Art

The key concept of the people's strength conferred a characteristic feature to the war as fought by the North, which was both a people's war and a total war; that is, the entire population participated in the war. The people were involved in all spheres; not only on the military front but on the economic, diplomatic, cultural and social fronts as well. Because war does not consist of purely military activities, the first principle of the military art is to combine armed struggle with political struggle; armed uprising with revolutionary warfare.

Here the North was clearly following Lenin's thesis that uprising and armed struggle are inseparable and indistinguishable in a people's war. It is no wonder then that even after the failure of the 1968 *Tet* Offensive, in which the expected "general uprising" of the people failed to materialize, North Vietnam continued to try to combine these two forms of struggle in their 1972 Summer Offensive and the 1975 Spring Offensive.

The second tenet of the military art is the application of the principle of strategic leadership and the importance of the rural areas. This tenet called for establishing a resolutely firm posture in rural areas from which to launch assaults on the Republic and the U.S. in three geographical domains: the mountains, the lowlands, and the cities, using tactics appropriate to each. This offensive scheme forces the adversary to spread himself thin, to become vulnerable to siege and attacks on all fronts, and prevents him from massing his strength.

The third tenet of the military art is the application of the principle offensive leadership. Communists consider revolution an offensive. Uprising is a form of offensive. Consequently, revolutionary warfare in the general sense is an offensive. The offensive has to take place in every locale. Even though at particular times and places the Communists were on the tactical defensive, these were construed as temporary, partial events; local defensives were assumed to create conditions and opportunities for fresh offensive. The defensive stance usually occurred in the initial stages of the war when Communists main forces needed protection and the guerrilla and regional forces carried the responsibilities for the military activities, attacking and harassing enemy areas to maintain the initiative.

The fourth tenet of the military art is aiming at greater and quicker victories while gearing up to a long struggle. The time factor in the long struggle is used to weaken and limit the enemy's power, allowing the Communists the opportunity to surmount their own problems with the conviction that the longer the struggle goes on, the weaker the enemy and the stronger the Communists will become. Thus a people's war is almost by definition a protracted war.

Attacks aimed at annihilating the enemy do not only mean destruction of his military power but of his political machinery as well. Just as the fundamental problem of war is the destruction of the enemy's military power, the fundamental goal of any revolution is the seizure of the government. Hence, the dismantling of the local government, the wresting of sovereign power and of the power to govern, are just as important as the annihilation of enemy military units. Such is the fifth tenet of the military art.

The sixth tenet, also not combined to purely military considerations, is concerned with securing international support, especially that of brotherly socialist nations, but all the while putting paramount importance of self-reliance. This tenet originated from the strategic concept of reliance on "the great rear", which is the Communist bloc, and on its support, even though this reliance was never a total one. Derived from this tenet was the idea that socialist esprit and solidarity occupy vital positions in war.

These six tenets of the military art were manifestly apparent in the strategy of North Vietnam. The ideas recurred even during discussions of military tactics, because to the North there was a close connection between strategy, campaigns, and tactics. A correct military strategy had to be able to engender conditions favorable to the successful realizations of campaigns and tactics. The military art must therefore create certain basic structures. These structures are:

(1) In a people's war, forces are stratified into three divisions: main forces, regular forces, and guerrillas. Coordination and employment of these forces constitutes an art that combines guerrilla warfare and conventional warfare in types of actions ranging from skirmishes through medium battles to large battles.

(2) Forces must constantly be on the offensive and the offensive uses all available forces, all available weapons in all forms and intensities at any place at any time.

(3) Ability must be developed to use a small force to fight a larger force. Small force must be so organized as to tackle the larger enemy from a position of strength and annihilate him.

(4) There must be a resolve to destroy. Destruction is more important than attrition. Not only the enemy's troops but also his war materiel and rear areas must be destroyed.

(5) In fighting the enemy, flexibility, determination, creativeness, and surprise must be achieved.

Of utmost importance is the employment of guerrilla warfare as part of military strategy as well as a strategic mission in the war. The transformation of guerrilla warfare to position warfare at the appropriate place and time must be planned for. No less important are accurate assessments of the situation, determination of the direction of attack, selection of methods of fighting, and the correct employment of forces. In addition, there must be developed an ability to evaluate accurately the overall balance of power between the two sides in terms of military as well as political strength, of quality as well as quantity, of strengths as well as weaknesses.

These five points are considered in strategic thinking, in the military art as well as in basic tactics. Beyond this, however, tactics have their own place. Generally speaking, the fundamentals of tactics are similar in all military forces, but their application does vary with the strategic conception of forms of warfare and the conduct of war.

Common Communist Tactics

In the initial stage, that is from 1960 to 1965, a common Communist tactic that inflicted significant losses on ARVN was the ambush. The ambush was a tactical maneuver carried out in accordance with the slogan "fight a small action to achieve great victory." There were six kinds of ambushes; ambush of small units, ambush of patrols, ambush of vehicular convoys, ambush of river crossings, ambush from underground positions, and ambush of mopping-up units.

One of the contributing reasons for Communist success in ambushes was first of all the habits of ambushed units. Often they were on road-clearing missions whose itineraries, times of departure and withdrawal, and forces involved rarely changed. The Communist took advantage of the boredom of the troops on these routine daily missions. So imbued were the ARVN practices in some areas that the enemy could use the same ambush sites repeatedly.

Ambush went hand in hand with attacks on outposts in a combination referred to as "assail the forts and strike the rescuers," according to which the "fort-assail" part more often than not yielded precedence to the "strike-the-rescuers" part.

Attacking outposts was one of the common activities of the Communists. Since outposts symbolized national authority, demolishing them would achieve both political and military advantages. No matter how strong a fort might be, it had the inevitable weaknesses of the fixed position, the defensive stance, the unchanged personnel strength, and limited firepower. The most widely employed technique against outposts was known as "one point, two faces," whereby a primary thrust was accompanied by two secondary ones.

Another tactic used against outposts was first shelling then assaulting. This came into increasing use after 1968 when Communist troops were better equipped with rockets and field artillery.

To wear down and delay the advance of the enemy, mines and booby traps were frequently employed. In fact, mines and booby traps caused the most ARVN losses in vehicles and personnel.

From 1969 on, sapper tactics received intense emphasis. The Communists, who pushed sapper employment to great lengths by regular sapper units and infantry units as well, used units from squad to regimental size. Sapper techniques received colorful names like "blooming amidst the enemy," or exotic ones like "deep in the heart," and were effective in raids and demolition actions against POL depots and other critical installations.

During the 1972 Summer Offensive, the Communist improved on their technique for blocking roads such as National Route 13 north of Chon Thanh. They dug deep, heavily fortified emplacements with communications tunnels and overhead cover that could withstand the heaviest bombs and artillery. They occupied these positions with only a squad of soldiers who were under orders to fight there for three days or until they were all killed. At the end of three days, the surviving members of the squad were replaced with a fresh squad from the company that occupied a covered, supporting position a few hundred meters to the rear in the dense jungle. Behind the company was the battalion, also dug in and prepared to prevent any attempt to bypass the road-block. This technique was extremely effective as well as economical in the use of troops.

Another technique for the defense of a critical position was developed to a high degree of effectiveness during the 1972 offensive. This was the siting of three mutually supporting fighting positions in such a way that their fields of fire interlocked to prevent any one position from being successfully assaulted. Of course, these positions could be defeated by determined, well-supported infantry assaults, but the costs were inevitably high.

Communist tactics were applied either in combination or in isolation. Tactics used singly were mostly sapper tactics because of the secrecy and isolation required.

Besides the common tactics, the Communists devised specific techniques to counter new techniques employed by U.S. and RVNAF forces. One family of techniques were those employed against helicopters. Helicopters at first caused tremendous trouble to Communist units with their speed and surprise. The Communists countered with poles planted at likely landing zones. Of course, this was only tokenism since it was impossible to plant poles in all likely landing zones. Communist units had to break up into small bands for concealment and mutual rescue, and had to have their mortars and artillery pre-adjusted on likely landing zones.

Helicopter vulnerabilities gradually became known: they were easy to shoot down, even with small arms, if they were hit in the engine. The fronts of helicopters thus became targets. A bullet was likely to hit either the engine or the pilot. Other weapons such as mines and anti-tank grenades were also employed against helicopters.

Defenses also had to be devised to deal with ARVN and U.S. armor. In the plains of the Third and Fourth Military Regions, and in the border areas between Cambodia and Vietnam, Communist troops were equipped with 57-mm and 75-mm recoilless rifles with which they could destroy armored personnel carriers at considerable ranges while B-40 and B-41 anti-tank grenades would destroy them at shorter ranges.

The Communists also wanted to capture ARVN armored vehicles for their own use. During their attack on Saigon in 1968, they directed a major effort towards the Armor Command at Go Vap to capture armored equipment to support the offensive. They tried again in 1972 when, north of Binh Dinh, they managed to capture six or seven M-113 armored personnel carriers.

The Communists also captured ARVN weapons and uniforms to disguise themselves as ARVN troops. In 1972 many successful attempts at disguise occurred, mostly in the Second Military Region, whose commanding general eventually ordered all troops in his command to wear steel helmets at all times. The measure succeeded because the Communist troops had taken no steel helmets.

In the long run, however, it was not the distinctive and ingenious Communist set of tactics that brought them the ultimate victory. Rather, it was the coherent, long-term, immutable devotion to a strategy that assumed, without question, that victory would come eventually to their side. Total war, people's war; it was one and the same. Their adversaries could not match this concept with any theory of war that they were prepared or willing to follow.

CHAPTER VIII

Observations and Conclusions

The military leaders of North Vietnam were strongly influenced by writings on the theory and art of warfare. One of the maxims they were fond of citing was this:

- When the tactics are wrong and the strategy is wrong, the war will be quickly lost;

- When the tactics are right but the strategy is wrong, battles may be won, but the war will be lost;

- When the tactics are wrong but the strategy is right, battles may be lost, but the war will be won;

- When both the tactics and strategy are right, the war will be won quickly.

During more than twenty years of war between the North and South, each side appeared to have the advantage from time to time. The South faced critical periods and tactical setbacks in 1964, 1968 and 1972 but each time its armed forces rebounded from the brink of defeat and caused the enemy to pull back and regroup. The Communist side suffered serious reverses in 1959, 1967, 1969, 1970 and 1971 but was able to recover to pursue its goal of conquest.

If one were to try to fit the maxim on tactics and strategy to the long conflict in Vietnam, one would probably agree that neither side had wrong tactics *and* wrong strategy, for if either side had been in this condition, the war would have been short.

What about the second case — right tactics and wrong strategy? If the theory is valid, perhaps one could conclude that South Vietnam's tactics were right at least some of the time since the South did win many battles. But the South lost the war; evidence that its strategy was faulty.

The third case is "wrong tactics; right strategy; victory at last." This might well apply to the North. No one could successfully demonstrate that all of the North's tactics were wrong, in fact many of them were very effective, but they did lose enough battles to suggest that their forces were on many occasions inferior to those of the South. But the maxim also suggests that the North's strategy was essentially correct. Success is the best proof of that conclusion.

A brief discussion of the opposing strategies and tactics will illustrate or refute the validity of the maxim as it has been applied to the Vietnam War. As far as tactics go, both sides knew how to improve and modify their own tactics to bring out their own particular strengths to the utmost and adjust to changing battlefield conditions. Deeply influenced by U.S. tactics and supplied with U.S. equipment, the RVNAF relied on the superiority of firepower, high mobility and abundant resources as the foundation of their tactics.

The Communist on the other hand, took advantage of their familiarity with the terrain, concealment and cover afforded by the terrain and the populace, attrition techniques, and the offensive advantages of mass and surprise. The prime Communist tactic, surpassing even sapper techniques, was the ambush. Eventually, however, ambush tactics were defeated by the counterambush measures which employed sophisticated techniques and hardware, coordination, and quick reaction by air, mechanized forces and artillery.

From a purely military point of view, South Vietnamese leaders improved their tactics and adapted them well to the operational requirements of the war. In contrast to the enemy, however, they failed to coordinate their tactics with their political goals. South Vietnamese units in combat usually were concerned only with military matters: the mission, means, enemy, and terrain. The mission nearly always referred to purely military objectives; little thought was given to the political results or side-effects of any operation. This insensitivity to political considerations at times resulted in actions condoned during combat operations which had adverse political effects, such as activities that resulted in the unnecessary loss of civilian lives or damage to their property. This was in stark contrast to Communist practice. Before embarking on an offensive, Communist cadres and troops studied and discussed the political aspects of the military operation and the tactics employed were designed with this in mind.

Nevertheless, throughout the war RVNAF and U.S. tactics enjoyed some remarkable successes and forced the enemy to make adjustments, devise countermeasures, and delayed his timetable for victory. For example, RVNAF and U.S. raids on the enemy's supply and infiltration routes compelled him to devote considerable combat resources to food production, route security, protection and reconnaissance for night movements, and alternate route construction. Likewise, with their helicopter mobility and heavy firepower, including the B-52s, the RVNAF and Americans conducted many successful attacks on the enemy's previously secure base areas, compelling him to defend in these rear areas, and to use men and other resources to repair damage, replace losses, and relocate facilities. Remarkable U.S. advances in communications intelligence means, some of which were also effectively employed by the RVNAF, forced the enemy to adopt communications systems much less efficient than radio and to keep his command posts moving lest they be accurately targetted for destruction.

The modern tactics and techniques introduced into Vietnam by the U.S. also had some significant effects on the way RVNAF soldiers and their units functioned in combat. The use of helicopters in the infantry assault spelled the end of the parachute assault which had been developed to a high degree of professionalism by the ARVN airborne units. But another more serious loss in overall combat efficiency and flexibility was directly caused by the reliance infantry units learned to place on externally provided heavy fire support. They became accustomed to the strikes of fighter-bombers, gunships, B-52s, and divisional artillery that would pound the objective before the assault. They forgot how to take an objective by stealth. They forgot how to use their own mortars, machine guns and recoilless rifles in close and continuous support of assaulting infantry.

They forgot how to maneuver for advantageous terrain in order to breach the weakest points of the enemy position.

After years of reliance on helicopters and trucks to move infantry to battle, units neglected the art of marching and with this neglect the troops became lazy; they were tough soldiers but they didn't really know the extent of their physical capabilities because they were so rarely tested.

The ARVN units fell into some other bad habits too. As field radios proliferated, few units bothered to use messengers or wire communications. Field encoding systems were either too much trouble to use — if they were relatively secure — or were too easily broken if they were easy to use. Consequently, great amounts of valuable, sensitive operational information was carelessly transmitted for the enemy to intercept. And he became quite good at it.

Eventually, after 1972, there was an end to the bountiful resources the RVNAF commanders could call upon. Not only were they suddenly deprived of the heavy American fire support that was critical to the survival of the nation's armed forces in the enemy's recent (1972) great offensive, but restrictions began to be placed on RVNAF's own mobility and firepower because of the decline in the American military assistance program. RVNAF commanders were not prepared to cope with this new austere environment. Why? Was it because the Republic still lacked a coherent, long-term strategy for winning? This appears to be the case.

Sun Tzu, the Chinese military philosopher wrote in his treatise on war: "The critical objective in war is to defeat the enemy's strategy."

The North's strategy was never a secret to the South. It was publicly discussed in the North Vietnamese press, appeared in articles and speeches by North Vietnamese leaders, and had been applied with success in the war between 1945 and 1954. There was no secret at all about its main elements: a long-term political struggle broadly based on the strength of the people, striking the enemy on all fronts. But it is one thing to know and another to find an antidote.

As one reviews and analyzes the South's search for a strategy to defeat the North's strategy, one is struck with the fact that the search was inhibited, perhaps fatally, by the factor of time. Time, the importance attached to quick solutions, and the limited time successive regimes — American as well as South Vietnamese — had available to find these solutions, pervaded all aspects of strategic thinking and planning.

A successful strategy must have continuity in time. This was never a problem in North Vietnam. Its leadership, military and civilian, was in office to stay until the strategy was pursued to its conclusive victory, much as America's and Great Britain's leadership remained in office all during World War II. This was not the case in South Vietnam. Its constitution required a presidential election every four years — as did America's — but its president was limited to only two successive terms (as America's was not in its great war). Furthermore, the institutions of republican government were not only undeveloped in South Vietnam when the war started, but were constantly under enemy attack. Governmental stability was denied the Republic of Vietnam, and governmental stability is a *sine qua non* for a coherent national strategy.

This perennial instability had another deleterious effect: it impelled the political leadership to develop personal followings and loyalties among the armed forces leadership, giving rise to factionalism, division of effort, *coup* plotting and rumors of the same, all of which contributed to wasteful and sometimes corrupt practices in the employment of military resources. Furthermore, military leaders often rose to positions of great responsibility because of political loyalty rather than because of military qualifications. Some of these leaders were militarily inept.

Another thing happened to South Vietnam's strategy: it became inseparable from the strategies the United States devised for the war. And the U.S. strategies were flawed by the same defect as the South Vietnamese: lack of continuity. Furthermore, U.S. policy prohibited a strategy shaped to achieve a real victory over the North. Some critics called it a "no win" strategy, but whatever it was, the U.S. strategy did not provide for a decisive defeat of the enemy.

South Vietnam's strategy did not begin that way. It started as an original, independent concept, quite removed from American influence. Until about 1963, South Vietnam's leaders were attempting to build a strong base of popular support upon which to form an effective military strategy that could defeat the enemy's broadly based, multifaceted campaign. Certainly the Americans influenced the structure of the South's armed forces during this period because the support for the entire effort was appropriated by the U.S. Congress and administered by the U.S. Defense Department. It seems regrettable that as early as 1954 the U.S Military Assistance Advisory Group failed to understand or appreciate the government's strategy; the MAAG opposed the force structure the government thought best suited for the execution of that strategy. With the Americans holding the purse-strings, neither the Vietnamese President nor the RVNAF General Staff could exert any significant influence on the military force structure or the military strategy from that time on.

The United States imposed a strategic limitaion upon itself, and consequently upon South Vietnam. Its strategic objective was to defeat the Communists in the South but not those in the North. Consistent with this strategic distinction, the United States provided South Vietnam with the means to defend its own territory but not to carry the war to the North. This limitation was, to the Communist theoreticians, a strategic absurdity.

The Americans entered the war with awesome power and advanced technology. It seemed that a happy division of labor could be arrived at. The U.S. forces would drive deep into the enemy zones and destroy his main forces while the RVNAF would confine its efforts to pacifying the populated areas. Despite the logic of this strategic decision, it had some serious faults. In the first place, the spectacular battles the Americans fought so well and with so much firepower and such large formations caught the eyes of all elements of the press. These battles became worldwide news. The tough, grinding, and largely successful pacification campaign the RVNAF were waging went largely unnoticed and unreported. The result was the unavoidable but erroneous impression that the Americans were doing all the fighting for the Vietnamese. This gave the Communistis more propaganda ammunition for their political war: "The Viet Cong were fighting the Americans to save Vietnam." It was a very effective line; it even convinced a lot of Americans.

Just as it appeared that the Americans had taken over the entire burden of the war from the South Vietnamese, so it appeared that the Vietnamese had abdicated all responsibility for strategic planning. Then came *Vietnamization*. All this would change and the Vietnamese would reassume the primary role for the prosecution of their own war. But it did not quite work out that way. *Vietnamization* really meant *Americanization*. The Vietnamese armed forces were deluged with new American war equipment in great quantities, from 175-mm guns and 90-mm gunned tanks to F-5 fighter-bombers. It was not possible to return (or revert) to a Vietnamese-style war. It was going to have to be fought the American way. This meant that firepower was the dominant element of the strategy. That was alright—for as long as the firepower was available and applied in the appropriate places at the right time.

The trouble was that the weight of the combat potential could never be brought to bear. After December 1972, the off-again, on-again American bombing strategy against North Vietnam ended for good and the strategy reverted to a South-only strategy. It shortly also became clear to all participants in the struggle that the crucial elements of the South's firepower advantage—U.S. air and naval power—would not be used. But South Vietnamese leaders were too slow to perceive these permutations in the overall strategy. The U.S. was gone. Left on their own, the Vietnamese leadership had no strategic alternatives available. Perhaps if they had better understood the workings of the American political system they would have been better prepared to deal with the new set of circumstances. But they mistakenly believed that the American President could keep his promises against the will of the American Congress. It was too late when they discovered the folly of this assumption.

Belatedly, President Thieu, in late 1974, began talking about fighting a "poor-man's war." It was too late to ask for this. There was no base of support for it. The political element of the national strategy had been ignored for too long in favor of the massive firepower and technological advantages that made politics almost irrelevant.

Another of Sun Tzu's maxims was "know yourself and know your enemy, and you will win a hundred victories in a hundred battles." The leadership of the Republic of Vietnam knew its enemy, but it knew neither itself nor its ally.

Glossary

ARVN	Army of the Republic of Vietnam
CG	Civil Guard
CORDS	Civil Operations and Revolutionary Development Support
COSVN	Central Office South Vietnam (Communist Headquarters)
DAO	Defense Attache Office
DIOCC	District Intelligence Operations Coordination Committee
GAMO	Groupe Administratif Militaire Operationel
GVN	Government of Vietnam
IOCC	Intelligence Operations Coordination Committee
JGS	Joint General Staff
MAAG	Military Assistance Advisory Group
MACV	Military Assistance Command Vietnam
NVA	North Vietnamese Army
PF	Popular Forces
PIOCC	Provincial Intelligence Operations Coordination Committee
PRU	Provincial Reconnaissance Unit
RF	Regional Forces
RVN	Republic of Vietnam
RVNAF	Republic of Vietnam Armed Forces
SEATO	Southeast Asia Treaty Organization
VC	Viet Cong
VCI	Viet Cong Infrastructure
VNAF	Vietnamese Air Force

www.ingramcontent.com/pod-product-compliance
Lightning Source LLC
Chambersburg PA
CBHW080513110426
42742CB00017B/3102